To: The Bridges

invite
PRESS

JESUS
UNCHAINED

JESUS UNCHAINED

How to Rise Above the Agendas, Find Peace, and Be Set Free

Robert Glenn Johnson

invite
PRESS

Plano, Texas

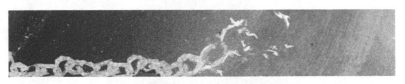

CONTENTS

Foreword — xi

PART I: WHO'S CHAINING WHOM?

Chain of Fools — 1

A Love Story — 10

Chained Reactions — 19

The Touchstone — 28

Organic Jesus — 35

Divine — 54

Human — 76

PART II: JESUS: THE CHAIN BREAKER

Mission — 97

Message — 115

New Life! — 131

Jesus Crowned — 150

A Closing Prayer: Take These Chains from My Heart — 157

"This is how we know we are in him: Whoever claims to live in him must live as Jesus did."

—*1 John 2:5b-6, NIV*

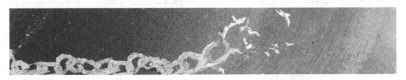

FOREWORD

I offer this book to you as a confession of faith and conviction that the story of Jesus is the most significant story ever told, that his is the most significant life ever lived, and that Jesus is the Truth that makes sense of life and our world

I have not come to that conclusion easily or quickly, but only through a long, arduous, adventurous journey that began in my childhood and has me now at the age of fifty-five.

I do not pretend that I have always been on the "right side" of Jesus on this journey. Over the course of my Jesus-journey, I have, at various times, hidden him, ignored him, suppressed him, rejected him, misunderstood him, misrepresented him, doubted him, and blamed him. I have, sometimes, even been his enemy. I have also had times when I celebrated, bore witness to, praised, defended, joyously studied, imitated, and by God's grace, followed Jesus. My journey has landed me at the conviction that Jesus is the Light of the world, as the Scriptures bear witness.

This book has been resonating in my being for two decades of my life. I have long wanted to share the truth of what I know about Jesus. I am glad that it is happening now. While I know that this witness to Jesus is incomplete, I also know what I would have said about Jesus 20 years would probably embarrass me a bit today. It may be the case that as I continue to learn more from and about Jesus, 20 years from now, I may cringe at what I have written here. Nevertheless, I hope that I have written a book that will, at least, provoke you to engage in your own adventure of discovering, learning about, and, maybe, hopefully, following Jesus.

I want to give a special thanks to my parents, who both taught and modeled Christian faith to my siblings and me. I give special thanks to the Friendship Community and Friendship Baptist Church, my childhood church, where I was further nurtured to value and pay attention to Jesus. I give thanks to St. Paul UMC in Laurel, MS, the church where I became a United Methodist while a college student at the University of Southern Mississippi. I thank Mt. Vernon UMC, Disciples UMC, Windsor Village UMC, and Aldersgate UMC. These faith communities allowed me to serve in leadership and were fertile grounds where my faith in Jesus could continue to grow. I thank Saint Mark UMC of Wichita, KS, for your trust and support, and I thank you for giving me the time and encouragement I needed to write.

I give my wife, Linda, and my daughters Giselle and Kayla very special thanks. They have known of my desire to write this book, which was envisioned, previously, with the title, "Blueprint Jesus." I used to carry my laptop on our annual vacations, promising to write. It never happened, and the idea of me writing a book on vacation, or at any time, eventually became a source of family humor. Yet here we are, and I could not have gotten here without your love, support, encouragement, and friendly meddling (lol).

The witness that I bear to Jesus in this book has two purposes: 1) I want to free Jesus' impact and love from "chains" of distortion and misrepresentation, and 2), I have tried to think, CREATIVELY, about how we can understand and bear witness to Jesus in our times. As you read this book, I don't expect you to agree with me about everything I present. Actually, I hope to unsettle you a bit in some of the ways you think about Jesus so that you will be open to seeing him in new, more precise, and more empowering ways. Instead of trying to answer all of your questions about Jesus, I hope you finish this book more determined than ever to keep learning about Jesus. He is worth every bit of the journey.

Robert Glenn Johnson
Wichita, Kansas
January 2022

PART 1

WHO'S CHAINING WHOM?

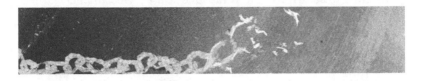

1
CHAIN OF FOOLS

Man is born free; and everywhere he is in chains.
—*Jean-Jacques Rousseau,* On the Social Contract[1]

They were the worst words I have ever heard someone say about Jesus. I have heard people say some very negative things about Jesus. Still, I had never in my life heard anyone say such hideous stuff about him as I was getting from a young man who happens to be very dear to me.

What bothered me most wasn't his rejection of everything that I knew he had learned about Jesus, but the expression of his rejection with such contempt and verbal ugliness. It wasn't just that he was denying that Jesus ever existed, or that he was asserting that people who believe in Jesus have placed their faith in a lie. It was that he laced his ideas with hatred and profanity. He wasn't merely rejecting Jesus. He was angry, and he was, most of all, hurt. Since he and I first began our ongoing conversations, I have come to see that his posture toward Jesus is connected to a growing sentiment about Jesus and Christianity across the world, especially in America.

Let's tell a hard truth. There is a massive gap between what Christians claim about Jesus and his actual influence in the world. That gap is the *demon* behind the words and disposition of this young man and the growing resentment, especially among young people, toward Jesus.

---

1. Jean-Jacques Rousseau, *On the Social Contract*, G.D. H. Cole, trans. (Augustine Press, 1923/2018), 12.

Jesus came to set us free. He is the One sent by God to liberate, heal, and restore us from the things that have blinded, broken, divided, and chained us. Yet, all over the world, it appears that Jesus' impact is impeded. Given what Jesus' followers believe and claim about him, why does he seem to have only a marginal impact upon not only the world but even those of us who call him "Savior"? Is Jesus chained?

Our claims about Jesus' identity and power are bold. We believe that, through his life, death, and resurrection, Jesus has redeemed fallen creation and reconciled the world back to God. We believe that Jesus lives within and through us who have, by grace, received Jesus into our lives and surrendered to him as Lord. We believe that Jesus is at work through us to fulfill his prayer that his Kingdom is fulfilled on earth (Matthew 6:10). We live confidently in Jesus' post-resurrection proclamation: "All authority has been given to Me in heaven and on earth." (Matthew 28:18).

Our celebration of Jesus and his power are pervasive. All over the world, people worship and celebrate Jesus. His name is on church buildings and church logos. He is studied, interpreted, and reinterpreted. His life and legacy fill the curricula of seminary classrooms. All over the world, people sing, preach, and teach about Jesus. Movements and wars happen in his name. *Gazillions* of dollars have been raised and spent in his name. He tops most lists of the most influential persons in human record. People have died for him and killed for him. His birth is the hinge of history for the most widely used calendar in the world (the Gregorian calendar). On the surface, it seems as if Jesus is everywhere, influencing everything. If we measure by size, power, wealth, and influence, it appears that Jesus and the Church are winning.

Yet, when we look deeper and longer, we see something entirely different. In this moment of history, the whole world is taking a deeper, more comprehensive look, facilitated by the enormous resources of 24-hour cable media and social media. As the world looks at Jesus and the Church, there is growing doubt about Jesus' relevance, power, and impact beyond the internal religious practices and beliefs of formal, institutional Christianity. Beneath the surface, there is deep trouble in the *paradise* of Christendom, and the world is asking us, the Church, some severe and substantive questions.

Some of these are the typical questions that have been raised for ages. If the risen Jesus is all-powerful and unlimited in love, why are so many things going wrong in the world and human history? Does Jesus care, or does he care but isn't able to do anything about these troubles? Why doesn't Jesus stop the senseless wars fought for no better reason than egos and lust for power or wealth? Why doesn't Jesus stop abortions? Why doesn't Jesus stop the school shootings that take the lives of innocent, helpless children? How did the Holocaust happen in a world where Jesus is the ultimate authority and power?

Where was Jesus during the chattel enslavement of Black Americans or the mass genocide of Native Americans? Why didn't Jesus protect the nine black Christians gathered to learn about him in the church in Charleston, South Carolina? Where is Jesus when some of the best people we know die, young, from cancer while some of the worst people we know prosper in every visible way? We could go on.

However, the most pressing questions these days are questions about how Christians, in general, are so far removed from the Jesus we read about in the Gospels. If *that* Jesus is now the risen Lord and lives through his followers, then why do we bear so little resemblance to him in our choices, behaviors, and lifestyles? Beneath our *church-ism* (songs, liturgies, meetings, revivals, conferences, life groups, ministries, offerings, collections, and beautiful buildings), it doesn't appear that we are genuinely formed and transformed by the character, values, mission, and passion of Jesus. Beneath *church-ism*, Christians are known the world over for being the best at some of the worst behaviors: hatred, war, judgmentalism, condemnation, racism, greed, and idolatries of all kinds.

For example, over the last half-century, the organization most known for being guilty of the sexual abuse of young boys is the Catholic Church. The absurd conspiracy theories of QAnon are rooted and nurtured in the American Protestant Church. Why? Why is it that in so many predominantly black communities, drugs and gang violence multiply despite a church on nearly every corner? How can these things be? It is one thing for Christians to misbehave. We are not perfect. It is quite another thing to become the hosts, curators, and protectors of evil, which we seem to be in so many cases. Where is Jesus? Why does his impact on us seem to be diminishing?

Many of Jesus' followers are very much like an adulteress wife visiting her lover with her husband's name tattooed on multiple places of her body. We wear the name of Jesus all over us while our lives, choices, values, and passions contradict our label.

And we are at war with each other. We are "a house divided against itself." We are more defined by and loyal to our political parties and political values than to Jesus and his Kingdom. We can worship together until it's election time. We can engage in mission work together until we discover that someone is a liberal or a conservative. We all wear Jesus' name but seem to desert him when he gets in the way of our social, cultural, economic, and political agendas, at which point, we are more than ready to—at worst—destroy each other and—at best—demonize each other. It seems that Jesus' claim on many of his followers is merely "skin-deep."

Christians don't seem to have even a broad consensus about what it means to be a Christian.

Over the past few years, as I have focused on the life and meaning of Jesus, I have informally polled Christians, curious to see how they think of and understand Jesus. I have asked people, "What does it mean to be a Christian?" Seldom did I get the answer that "being a Christian means to be a follower of Jesus."

I have served on boards of ordained ministry in The United Methodist Church. It is surprising how many candidates I helped interview who could not adequately answer this question: "What is the central claim of the Christian faith?" They didn't give bad answers, but many of them didn't know that the central claim of the Christian faith is "Jesus Christ is Lord." Many of them were nearly clueless about what it is that essentially defines us as Christians.

A good friend of mine, a pastor, tried to explain the results I was getting. "Until recently," she said, "following Jesus or Jesus being Lord over my life had never occurred to me in my decision to be a Christian. For most of my life, including after joining a local church, I thought that being a Christian meant joining a Christian community, going to worship services every week, participating in a Bible study, tithing, and being a morally good person. Becoming like Jesus, imitating Jesus, letting Jesus live his life through me was not in my consciousness." She went on to say, "I'll bet that my experience is true for most people who call themselves Christians." If we measure her assertion by the depth of Jesus' actual influence on Christians (and the world), I'll bet that she's right.

Observing our behavior as Christians, it is as if we have taken Jesus' name and identity and are using them in ways foreign to who Jesus was and is.

Personal-identity theft has always been a threat, but with the onset and exponential growth of the internet, it has become common and normalized. Through a host of methods and strategies, thieves can steal your identity and act in the world as if they are you. Using your identity, they might do anything from making false unemployment claims to creating credit lines and running up illegitimate debt. These people adopt your identity and then do all kinds of evil as you.

It is not outrageous to assert that Jesus' identity has been taken over and perverted so much so that, in many circles of the Church, the Jesus presented is a dark caricature, grotesque imitation, or complete misrepresentation of who Jesus really was and is. Those circles of the Church are perpetrating "spiritual crimes" in the name and person of Jesus.

False Renditions of Jesus

As false versions of Jesus have multiplied, they are like chains imposed on Jesus' impact, repressing, restraining, and restricting his influence on all of creation. What's more, the caricatures of Jesus come in many shapes and sizes. In America, alone, there is a host of perverted versions of Jesus.

There's the *jesus* who has been stripped of any of the physical attributes of his actual ethnicity and culture and portrayed as a white, blond-haired, blue-eyed European, which, of course, doesn't matter, unless it matters.

There's *jesus*, the American nationalist, who is always pro-American and who leads his followers to assert and protect the primacy of America over all the world by any means necessary. Furthermore, what these *jesus* followers love most about him is that they never have to question if *jesus* is on their side. They can always assume and be confident that he is.

There's the white supremacist *jesus*, defender, sustainer, and symbol of white colonialism and white privilege. He led the charge in the genocide, oppression, enslavement, desecration, and colonizing of Native Americans. He permitted the purchase, transportation, and chattel enslavement of Africans. He inspired the creation of the Ku Klux Klan. He signed the postcards that white hate-mobs created to send to friends when they lynched innocent Black Americans. He cares deeply for the pain and suffering of white Americans but has no compassion for the suffering of persons of color. At times in American history, he has infiltrated the white Church to give religious sanctioning of white violence and hatred.

There's the black militant *jesus*, whose followers live their lives and build their theological perspectives more as angry reactions to white racism than as hope-filled responses to God.

There's the *jesus* who has become the "god of greed and materialism," who measures everything, including success and the quality of people's faith, by market value and wealth accumulation. This *jesus* even shows up in many churches, inspiring the "name-it-and-claim it" prosperity gospel and guiding other followers to measure the impact of churches by the size of their sanctuaries and other church buildings.

There are more:

- the *jesus* of relentless individualism, for whom everything is a private matter

- the spiritual *jesus*, who has no interest in changing his followers' circumstances

- the heavenly *jesus*, whose only concern is what will happen to people after they die

- the various versions of an emotionally vague *jesus*, who is always mad, sad, passive, or boring

- the *jesus*, who was concerned only about matters of established religion

- the *jesus*, who is just a moral teacher or rebel Jewish philosopher

- the *jesus*, whose only value and significance is his crucifixion

- the *jesus*, who was human in appearance only (Docetism lives on)

- the *jesus*, who lived without struggle or challenge

- the *jesus*, who would never cause conflict

- the *jesus*, who is available only for Christians, the Church, and those people who are willing to conform to the

Church's moral and cultural codes of conduct

- the *jesus*, who exists only inside of a church-building
- the denominational *jesuses*, (Baptist, Methodist, Pentecostal, etc.)

The list of false *jesuses* is endless, with every subculture of American society conceiving and forging its own version of Jesus: Democrats, Republicans, Conservatives, Liberals, promoters of guns, and promoters of social welfare. Name an extreme in America, and you can bet that there's an associated *jesus*, who cultivates a version of Christianity that serves it.

I have mentioned only the distortions of Jesus deriving from people who have a positive disposition toward him. There are also numerous *jesuses* created and defined by people who despise the person, story, and even the idea of Jesus.

Of course, the forging of false *jesuses* is not an action unique to America. It happens worldwide, wherever the story of Jesus is known and where people attempt to apply the story of Jesus to how they live their lives.

My quick mention of these renditions of Jesus is not by way of a casual dismissing of their impact and influence. There is real power in these distortions because they have a bit of truth connected to them; in this era, you don't need a whole truth to be convincing to the masses. A bit of truth wedded to a lot of unbridled passion has proven capable of launching revolutions, toppling governments, overturning long-established traditions, and collapsing economies.

The young man I mentioned in the beginning was rejecting a caricature of Jesus and not Jesus as he truly is. He was angry with a *jesus* who:

- has white hair and blue eyes
- is a creation of white American slave owners
- supported slavery and the destruction of Black people
- took his mom from him, unfairly
- doesn't answer prayer
- identifies with white supremacy

- is a puppet-tool of the Black Church to take advantage of Black people
- probably never existed, and if he did is, most certainly, dead.

His kind of resentment happens when the Church doesn't tell the truth about Jesus and instead creates versions of him that support our addictions, dark passions, and twisted agendas.

So, although Jesus is known all over the world, the numerous distortions of him have significantly impeded his impact. **He came to set us free, yet his influence and impact seem to be hindered, opposed, and stifled everywhere. It is as if his impact is in chains.** Those of us who love him and follow him, who still believe that he is the Light of the world, need to engage in a relentless effort to remove the barriers to Jesus' influence that we have erected and *re-present* him to the world, *unchained* from the confusing, perverted renditions of him. We must bear witness to Jesus with less distortion and with greater clarity.

I once dreamed that I was walking through a forest with a pastor who remains one of my mentors. As we made our way through the thick forest, we started seeing giant snakes in the trees. Suddenly afraid, we began to sprint to get out of the woods, but the snakes began falling out of the trees, and one of them fell on my mentor and started wrapping itself around him. He broke free, but just as he did, another snake fell on him, and then another one, and another one. I stood there, locked in terror, wanting to help him but feeling helpless. As the snakes were enveloping him, I turned to start running to save my own life.

The next day, I reached out to a good friend of mine, a prayer warrior whose counsel I deeply trusted, and asked him to help me interpret that dream. He told me that the dream meant that my mentor would come under a spiritual attack and that, when it happens, I was to "stay in the forest" and help him get free. I took his interpretation as a helpful one, but I felt that there was more.

Now, I think that dream is about a lot of things and a lot of people. I think that evil *snakes* are wrapping themselves around a lot of God's people and squeezing out God's blessings. I know that there are times in my life when I am the one on whom the snakes are falling, and I need people to help me get free.

Jesus is being attacked by *snakes* of distortion, misrepresentation, and unbelief. Of course, these snakes can't get to Jesus himself, but they are wrapping themselves around his influence, choking the strength out of his impact in the world.

As my prayer-warrior friend counseled me years ago, I will stay in the fight and the faith, and as Jesus lives through me, bear witness to the *true* Jesus, to help the influence and sway of Jesus in the world break free from the snakes of distortion and misrepresentation.

This book is one attempt to aid in the work of setting Jesus' influence free. In this book, I'll attempt to present a holistic picture of Jesus as he is witnessed to in the Bible, especially the four Gospels, with the ultimate goal of helping us to *see* him, encounter him, and be transformed by him.

The truth is that it isn't Jesus who is chained; we are. Our idolatries, wicked agendas, and selfish ambitions have chained us and made us unable to embrace Jesus' presence and power. I pray that this book will help us see our idolatries and show us a clearer picture of Jesus. Maybe if we can see Jesus clearer and better, we will fully embrace him and allow him to transform us into the beautiful beings God created us to be!

Before we turn to the Bible and work toward a holistic vision of Jesus, I must tell you why I love Jesus and why I believe he's "worth fighting for." He is not only the Light of the world; he is the Light of my heart.

2
A LOVE STORY

*In pain, I'd rather walk with Jesus with all of my questions,
than walk by myself with all of my answers.*

—*Rick Warren*[1]

I was born into a Christian family and raised in the Church. I have
had a long, complex, adventurous, multifaceted, and ever-evolving
relationship with Jesus. At times, I have been his enemy. I have spent
most of my adult life learning to love him and advocating on his behalf.
He has won my loyalty with his relentless, faithful love demonstrated
over a wide-ranging spectrum of experiences. You could say that I have
come to know and love him with my heart, mind, soul, and strength.
Jesus has saved me many times and in many ways throughout my life. I
want to tell you about five of those times.

Monsters in the Dark

The first time Jesus saved me, I was just a kid. I was super afraid
of the dark. Growing up in a small, FHA home in the hills of southern
Mississippi, I slept in the same bed with my brother, which was perfect
in my mind, because I was convinced that there were monsters waiting
to get me, who needed me to be in the dark long enough for them to
attack.

On one occasion though, my brother became sick with the flu. As
a result, my mother ordered me to sleep on the couch, in the den, in

1. Rick Warren, Facebook post, April 19, 2013.

the dark, *alone*! After everyone was in bed, I got up, turned on the hall light, and went back to the couch, feeling some sense of comfort. A few minutes later, my mother came into the den, clearly upset with me, and said, "stay on the that couch and don't turn this hall light back on!" She turned off the light, returned to her bedroom, and there I was, on the couch, no big brother, and no light. I was terrified. Being raised in a Christian home, I remember praying and asking God to protect me.

I can't tell you if what happened next was real or just my mind, tormented by fear, finding a way to survive this moment. Extreme fear can do extreme things to our minds. As I lay there praying, I opened my eyes and saw in the swallowing darkness a gray-colored hand, floating slowly down from the ceiling. As I looked closer, I noticed that the hand was pierced and bleeding in the palm. I took that to mean that it was the hand of Jesus. Had I not been in a Christian home, I would have probably interpreted that hand to be the hand of Frankenstein. The hand drifted down toward the floor, very slowly. A kitchen counter would have prevented me from being able to see it touch the ground, but by the time it got as far down as the countertop, a surprising peace had overtaken me, and I fell fast asleep. When I awakened, the night and the darkness were gone. It was morning.

Did I really see the hand of Jesus? Or was it my mind creating a reality to help me get through a moment of immense and overwhelming fear? Who can really know? Real or not, the presence of Jesus, as I had come to know him through my Christian home and childhood church, saved me from the darkness and its hidden monsters.

Cassandra's Anointing

The second time Jesus saved me also happened in my childhood. On this occasion, my eldest sister was struggling for life from a severe asthmatic episode. She had been taken to the ER and then sent home by doctors who had told my parents that they had reached the limit of what they could do for her.

My maternal grandfather was at our home for one of his long-term visits. He usually visited two or three times a year. He was a person of faith, a licensed preacher in the Church of God in Christ denomination, and he had his anointing oil with him. He had that oil with him at all times. As my other siblings and I got the news from our parents about my sister's prognosis and went to our bedrooms, my grandfather, affectionately referred to as *Paw-Paw*, went into the room where my eldest sister was struggling to breathe. The sounds of my sister struggling to breathe and of her spraying the medicinal inhaler are sounds that I will never forget.

As my grandfather started his prayer and oil-anointing of Cassandra's chest, my older brother looked at me and made a suggestion: "Maybe if we give our hearts to him, Jesus will let Cassandra live. Let's get on our knees right now and give our lives to Jesus." We got down on our knees and prayed the prayer of salvation that we had learned about and heard many times in our little Baptist church. "Jesus, I confess that I am a sinner. I repent of my sins. I ask you to come into my life and be my Lord and Savior. Then, we added an extra line: "And Jesus, please, let Cassandra live."

When we woke up the next morning, we got up and went into the Cassandra's room. She was alive and sleeping peacefully.

Did Cassandra live because of our prayers and Paw-Paw's anointing oil? Who can really know? In my mind, Jesus saved my sister from dying as a teen and saved my family from devastating loss and grief.

My Great Awakening

My third Jesus experience really combines several stories in one. The first happened in college at the University of Southern Mississippi. As a young man aspiring to be a pastor, I took a philosophy of religion course. The goal of the professor seemed to be the philosophical debunking of Christianity and all belief in God. To be fair, for every debunking argument, he gave opposing arguments, but the arguments in defense of Christianity were not given with the same degree of creativity and passion. After spending the entire semester debunking Christianity, he left us with two "seeds of hope."

First, he told us that, if we believe in God and live according to the Bible, but there's no afterlife, then we haven't lost anything; at least we lived good lives that brought us some measure of peace and purpose. However, if we are right, and there is an afterlife with both a heaven and a hell, and we have believed in God and lived our lives according to what God has commanded in the Bible, then we got it right, and we will spend eternity in heaven. "So," he resolved, "I suppose there's nothing too bad about being a believer, so long as you aren't using religion to hurt others."

Second, he suggested that "although Jesus probably isn't real, the character presented in the biblical stories is for the most part as much of a healthy model for life as anything else. You won't do too badly at life if you imitate many of the things Jesus says in the Gospels," he said.

I'm not sure if the professor meant to be comforting or encouraging. I seriously doubt it. Yet, that second suggestion gave me hope. If none of the other things I had been taught to believe made sense, Jesus made sense. At least he was worth imitating and following.

My childhood pastor and another older pastor from my hometown, with whom I had built a relationship, had been encouraging me through that intellectual and spiritual storm with a singular counsel: "Hold on to what you have experienced and learned about Jesus." At this point in the journey, Jesus was all I had; as I *stood* on the brink of an abyss of unbelief and cynicism, Jesus rescued me.

Later, the nihilism of that college semester returned a bit during my journey through Perkins School of Theology, as I encountered for the first time, things like the historical-critical method of interpreting the Bible, the "demythologizing" method of theologian Rudolph Bultmann, and the comprehensive history of Christianity. Learning about the events that shaped the story and theologies of the Church can be a staggering and overwhelming experience. At the end of my sojourn through Perkins School of Theology, I still had faith in Jesus. He was for me, a bit demythologized, but I was committed to being a partner with him in a ministry of social-justice advocacy through the vehicle of The United Methodist Church. I left Perkins with Jesus the liberator.

Then God did a thing. I was appointed to a megachurch in Houston, Texas, which exhibited an eccentric blend of Wesleyan revivalism, United Methodist structure, Baptist fundamentalism, Pentecostal passion, and liberation theology, all held in creative tension through the brilliance of Kirbyjon Caldwell, a Wharton Business School grad and former Wall Street banker. I started encountering Jesus in new, riveting, and sometimes frightening ways. Slowly, I started to become *unchained*—in my heart and mind—from the bonds of an unforgiving theological liberalism.

Now, I greatly valued the intellectual rigor I had developed at Perkins. Schubert Ogden and other professors there had met a need I had to pursue intellectual integrity even in my spirituality and faith. I easily embraced what Methodists refer to as the Wesleyan Quadrilateral as a way of assessing the validity of Christian witness and action: scripture, tradition, experience, and reason. For me at that time, reason protected me from the fundamentalism of my childhood and what I thought of as the unusual things I was seeing in the brand of Pentecostalism I was encountering at the megachurch in Houston. Reason meant that Christian witness and practice, from a sermon to an attempt at community outreach, had to make logical sense. Reason meant that I was to love God with my mind as well as my emotions and beliefs. And then, the final *coup d'é·tat* happened.

The first time I heard Bishop Veron Ashe preach, I went through a kind of *deliverance* from all the theological boxes and religious absurdities I had experienced in my journey. Bishop Ashe was the strangest man and preacher I'd ever met. He had grown up in the West Indies with a wealthy, Catholic mom who would leave him in the care of a black nanny. The nanny, a Pentecostal, would take Veron with her to church, and he would experience Black Pentecostalism in its fullness. However, when he grew up, he rejected the Pentecostalism he experienced, returned to his Catholic roots, eventually ending up in the Syrian Orthodox Church. He had found a way to combine his Catholic roots with all its regal liturgy and ceremony with his Pentecostal experiences of the Holy Spirit. To that he added intellectual rigor and a relentless pursuit of integrity in the interpretation of Scripture.

Veron Ashe was a combination of all my favorite *manifestations* of Jesus. He had the communicative gifts of a Southern, Black, Baptist preacher, the fervor of a Pentecostal/Charismatic, the intellectual rigor of a Perkins professor, the merging of revivalism with social ministry like John Wesley, the theological passion of a Schubert Ogden, the theological creativity of a Leonard Sweet, and the sacramental devotion of the Catholics and Orthodox churches of the East, all dressed in the garments of Syrian Orthodoxy!

He *re-presented* Jesus to me, and this was Jesus in all the dimensions that he is presented in the Gospels. I could be Christian again. I could be Methodist again. I could return to the roots of my childhood, although I would return as a new being, *unchained*. I could be both traditional and contemporary. I could be contemplative and outwardly expressive. I could shout over intellectual rigor. I could see as never before that I was called to attend to both people's hearts and their social circumstances. It all made sense. Jesus was "back" for me, and I was "born again."

Along with Kirbyjon Caldwell, Windsor Village, and Veron Ashe, this new awakening to Jesus was cultivated and nurtured by others, such as Jeremiah Wright. Most Americans came to know of Jeremiah Wright during the first presidential campaign of Barack Obama, when Rev. Wright himself was severely chained by misperceptions and distortions when he became a political tool against Obama's presidential bid. Despite how he was being misconstrued in the media, millions of Christians across the country knew him to be an uncompromising evangelical and brilliant scholar who did three things very well: he defended Christianity against intellectual liberalism, he defended Christianity against the unfounded accusations of irrational black militancy, and he was an unapologetic defender and celebrator of Jesus. His church's mission statement was a call for the congregation to be "unashamedly black and unapologetically Christian." I would listen to Jeremiah Wright's sermons over and over, and the more I listened, the more I regained my faith in Jesus as he is presented in the Gospels.

Through these persons and many others, Jesus was resurrected in my mind and my heart. Jesus had saved me from an abyss of unbelief and nihilism.

Confronted by Death

Often, saving comes from struggle. My fourth encounter with Jesus' saving grace happened when I was forty-one years of age during yet another time of struggle. I had been pastoring full-time for fifteen years. The sister whose sickness had inspired me to surrender to Jesus in my childhood had died at the age of forty-six, not from asthma, but from sarcoidosis, a brutal disease that randomly attacks the organs of the body until the body is ravaged with the leftover effects of physical trauma. This was one of the darkest moments in my life, and the darkness was fully realized at her grave site, when they began to lower her body into the grave. I began to think about how my sister had been sick all her life, struggling for breath. I thought about how she had been poorly served by a health care system that focused on her asthma and diagnosed the sarcoidosis too late. I thought about how, during a visit with her in the hospital, she asked me to read to her from Psalm 118:17, "I shall not die, but live, And declare the works of the LORD." Now, her body was being lowered into a grave, and it all seemed so . . . FINAL.

Holding my youngest sister's hand, I fell apart, emotionally overwhelmed by anger, grief, and despair. In my head, I said to God, "Really, Lord? Is this how my sister's life ends? Is this how it ends for all of us, a stiff body being lowered into a dirt hole? She loved you. She trusted you, and this is what she gets at age forty-six? This can't be the end of the story." And then, a switch. Much like the psalms of lament, my plea moved from lament to hope. "God, please, don't let this be the end. God, please don't let this be her end, our end. Let your word be true. Let Jesus be true when he said, "I am the resurrection and the life. Anyone who believes in me will live, even after dying" (John 11:25, NLT).

Jesus would save me again, but not in that moment. In the grief of my sister's death, I almost fell back into the abyss of cynicism and despair, but as I left her grave site, I left with a new commitment to do all I could to explore the life, meaning, potential, and promise of Jesus, and in that journey of this new commitment, all soaked in God's grace, I have grown into a firm, yet flexible confidence that Jesus is indeed the Light of the world.

Witnessing Resurrection

After my sister's death, I began a new journey of faith. That journey has given me the depth to live through a fifth struggle, a current and contemporary battle with nihilism. This battle has been provoked by the presidency of Donald Trump, and while I have passionate opinions about President Trump, he is not my focus here. Trump's presidency exposed, like almost nothing since American slavery, the hypocrisy and deep divisions in the body of Christ in America. The different segments of the Church in America agree on almost nothing. We don't agree on what it means to be a Christian. We don't agree on the mission of the Church. We don't agree on the meaning of Jesus. We don't agree on fundamental doctrines and theological principles. We don't agree on what it means to be filled with the Holy Spirit. We don't agree on how much weight social justice should have in our lives and work as God's people. We don't agree on how to measure the validity of Christian life and witness.

The Church in America has always been divided. Yet the divisions now are much more than denominational or doctrinal. We are multiple, radically different faiths, all wearing the same label. This deep division has caused many American Christians to leave the Church, denounce the label of Christianity, and doubt the truthfulness and trustworthiness of the Christian faith.

This divisiveness has caused even me to entertain serious doubts about whether any of us are truly surrendered to the Jesus we call Lord. We can't even agree on how to begin a conversation about how to live out our faith in the public sphere. How do we then tackle the more serious problems of our time?

Why am I still a Christian? I hold on to hope for a resurrection of faith in America and throughout the world. Beneath the dogmas, the doctrines, the divisions, the dark developments of our era, the delusions, the derisions, and the dissolutions of the Church in America, there is Jesus, and he makes sense. My philosophy of religion professor from college was onto something. Jesus can give rhyme, reason, and rhythm to our chaotic and confused efforts to be fully human.

For a year-and-a half, I served a predominantly white, United Methodist congregation in College Station, TX. College Station is in south central Texas, a deeply conservative region in a politically conservative state. Yet Aldersgate UMC was something else. The people of Aldersgate were political and social conservatives for the most part, but they were also complex. A lot of them were either engineers or professors in other academic disciplines. They were United Methodists. They represented multiple races and ethnicities. There were wealthy people and people who were barely surviving economically. And they were charismatics. In loving jest, I would refer to the people of Aldersgate as a *rag-tag* bunch of Jesus-lovers, a hodge-podge of Jesus-loving, charismatic intellectuals.

One guy, an engineer, definitely a political conservative, was vehemently opposed to liberal ideologies and progressive social policies. Yet he had a loving spirit. One Sunday, he showed up at a worship service of a black congregation who were leasing a building from him and had fallen behind on their lease payments. When he arrived, he saw that his presence aroused fear among them. They assumed that he was there to take back their keys. Instead of taking the keys, at the end of the service, he got up, held up the lease, and tore it to shreds. He told them that Jesus had instructed him to give them the building, and then he danced with them in jubilation all over the sanctuary. That wasn't social welfare. That was Jesus liberating a congregation from financial debt and obligation, so they could be free to redirect their resources toward ministry and mission. Now they could focus on introducing Jesus to the people of the Bryan/College Station region.

When I saw the radical diversity among the people of Aldersgate, and when I considered what it would take to bring us together into a unified family who could give singular witness to God's goodness in that area, I went to the one thing that had always rescued me in moments of profound challenge. I preached an extended series entitled, "Blueprint Jesus," which claimed that Jesus is the key to understanding humanity, God, and the meaning of life and all of creation.

I don't know how effective my preaching was in that series, but I can say that we all made a connection with one another in Jesus. The connection was confirmed for me when, after worship one Sunday, a young adult approached me and said, "Pastor, thank you for this series on Jesus. Really, I mean it. I come from a religiously abusive home. I saw a lot of religious hypocrisy too. People acted one way on Sundays at the church building but an entirely different way in our home. I was about to give up on Christianity, but now I have new hope. I have new meaning as a Christian. Jesus, the real Jesus whom you have been presenting, has saved my faith." I could most definitely identify with this young adult woman. Jesus had saved my faith too, over and over again.

I am hoping that, as you read the rest of this book, and as you journey with me in your faith, you too can allow Jesus to free you from the chains of the personal and cultural distortions, perversions, caricatures, and misinterpretations that have bound you; that you will see the living, saving Jesus as he truly is, and will know, again or maybe for the first time, that Jesus is the Light of the world and your one and only savior.

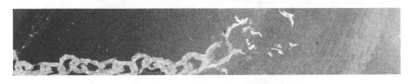

3
CHAINED
REACTIONS

*The worst tragedy for a poet is to be admired
through being misunderstood.*

—*Jean Cocteau*[1]

A s I have been writing this book, I have been asked repeatedly, "So what is your book about?" About half the time, when I give the title, I get a response of concern, confusion, or consternation. If the conversation happened in person, concern was expressed through a facial expression that said, basically, "What?!!" Most church folks have what theologians refer to as a "high Christology," an understanding of a fully divine Jesus with all the competencies and qualities of God, including omnipotence. So, if Jesus is omnipotent, how can I speak of a chained impact of Jesus? This is a great question. Is there biblical grounding to speak of Jesus or his impact being impeded, restricted, blocked, or chained?

Early Success

The Gospels of Matthew and Mark both report a startling story not found in either Luke or John. The story, along with its meanings and

---

1. Jean Cocteau, "Le Coq et l'Arlequin," *Le Rappel à l'Ordre* [*Recall to Order*] (Paris: Paris librairie Stock 1926), p. 20.

implications, is surprising and riveting. Follow the story with me and pay attention to how his ministry builds momentum.

According to Mark, Jesus proclaimed that the Kingdom was near and demonstrated the power of the Kingdom (Mark 1–5). In addition to his powerful teaching ministry, Jesus cast out demons with a simple command and healed many people who were suffering from sicknesses and diseases, including a leper, whom he touched and cleansed without himself getting infected (Mark 1:40-44).

He healed a paralyzed man through the faith of the man's friends, almost as if to say, "In any situation, I just need *someone* to believe, and nothing will be impossible. This man doesn't have faith? I see the faith of his friends. That will do" (see 2:1-12).

At one point, in these early days of his ministry, after he had healed Peter's mother-in-law, Mark says, "the whole city was gathered together at the door" (1:33) of Peter's home, and their faith and expectancy became an entrance for the power of God's Kingdom, as manifested in and through Jesus, to enter their lives in restorative and miraculous ways.

As Jesus built his school of disciples, with only a simple command, he successfully called people to leave their life-sustaining work and follow him (Mark 1:16-20; 2:13-14).

According to Mark's Gospel, demons were fully aware that Jesus had authority over them. They cried out a request for Jesus not to bother them: "Leave us alone! What have we to do with you, Jesus of Nazareth? Did you come to destroy us? I know who you are—the Holy One of God!" (Mark 1:24; see also 3:11-12).

As the crowds heard about his miraculous deeds, they began following Jesus from Galilee, Judea, and Jerusalem to Idumea beyond the Jordan and even to Tyre and Sidon, seeking healing and deliverance. The crowds were getting so large that Jesus was concerned about getting crushed by them (Mark 3:9).

As the work of teaching, healing, and delivering overwhelmed him, Jesus appointed twelve of his *believing* followers to go and do the same ministries that he had been doing. Mark highlights that, right there, among the twelve, was "Judas Iscariot, who also betrayed Him" (Mark 3:19). It was as if Mark was saying, "Even Judas believed, and he believed enough to go out and do the same miracles that Jesus had been doing."

As his ministry spread, Jesus was cultivating and responding to be-lief wherever he went.

However, let us hit *pause* on our journey of examining the expan-sion and popularity of his ministry to make note of four exceptions. Jesus was not faring well with the Jewish scribes and Pharisees (see Mark 2:6-8, 15-16, 23-24), the disciples of his cousin John the Baptist (2:18), the Herodians (3:6), and his family.

Foretelling what was on the horizon for Jesus and his ministry, in Mark 3:21, Mark tells us, "His family heard about all these things. They went to get him because people said he was crazy" (ERV). Eventually, Jesus arrived on the scene, and was told that his family was looking for him. According to Mark, this is how Jesus responded to the news that his family was looking for him:

> But He answered them, saying, "Who is My mother, or My brothers?" And He looked around in a circle at those who sat about Him, and said, "Here are My mother and My brothers! For whoever does the will of God is My brother and My sister and mother" (3:33-35).

Jesus' response to his family seems harsh, unless you understand it in relation to the likelihood that he knows, through word of mouth or discernment, about their interpretation of his ministry.

We'll pick up this narrative in a moment. For now, hit *play*, and let us continue our examination of how Jesus' ministry is expanding and building momentum. In Mark 4:35-41, we are told that nature yields to the authority and power coming from and through Jesus. As Mark puts it on the lips of the disciples, "even the wind and the sea obey him!" Wow.

However, we find out that his disciples, who had at first believed and followed him without hesitation, now struggle to maintain belief in a storm. Note that, how this storm episode impacted his "once-quick-to-believe-disciples" was not missed, at all, by Jesus. Later, he will revisit what this story reveals.

In chapter 5 of Mark, we find further demonstrations of the King-dom's power in and through Jesus. Demons and nature yield to him. They believe in the power coming from him. A legion of demons cast out of a man ask Jesus for permission to enter a herd of swine. They un-derstand that this power and authority coming through Jesus has com-mand over them.

The early, rapid, and successful expansion of this first phase of Jesus' ministry climaxes with two miraculous healings, both connected to powerful demonstrations of faith and belief. A ruler of the local synagogue by the name of Jairus ignores the increasingly negative sentiment against Jesus that is developing among his fellow Jewish leaders. Showing extraordinary faith and courage, he goes to Jesus, falls on his knees, and begs Jesus to come to his house to heal his sick daughter. Jesus responds immediately.

On the way to Jairus's home, with a crowd of people following him, reaching to get close to him, Jesus turns around and asks, "Who touched my clothes" (v. 30b)? His question makes no sense to his disciples because, as far as they could tell, he was being touched by lots of people. The touch that made him stop and turn around, however, was different. It was the touch of someone who was demonstrating extraordinary belief. In Luke's telling of this story, Jesus says, "Somebody touched me, for I perceived power going out from me" (Luke 8:46). Someone had such belief that it pulled power from Jesus' being, through his clothes. It was a woman who had been bleeding to death for twelve years, but from her touch of Jesus' garments, was immediately healed. What was happening in this moment? Jesus says to the woman, "Daughter, your faith has made you well" (v. 34b).

This story demonstrated that Jesus was carrying the power and authority of the Kingdom in his bosom, and it could be accessed and leveraged by faith. The woman's healing was not the result of just her faith or just the power embodied in Jesus but a dynamic interaction between the two. We know that Jesus sometimes heals people as an act of pure grace, but in this story, he heals in response to faith.

Now we arrive at Jairus's house and Jesus heals his daughter in response to Jairus's faith. Mark tells us that Jesus, after witnessing the "commotion" (v. 39) of the weeping crowd gathered at Jairus's home, and encountering ridicule from those same weeping bystanders, Jesus "put them all outside," and then healed Jairus's daughter. Was Jesus' action of putting the weeping crowd out of Jairus's home implying that the healing that he wanted to execute might be hindered by an atmosphere of unbelief created by the collective unbelief of the crowd? Maybe. What happens next might help us answer this question.

He Could Do No Deeds of Power

Jesus departs Galilee and goes to Nazareth, his hometown. On the ensuing Sabbath, he goes to the local synagogue and teaches. Jesus is home, among the people who knew him first and best. They are astounded, surprised, and puzzled, but most of all, Mark says, they are offended (v. 3). Jesus has had sway with leprosy, withered hands, disease, paralysis, and even demons and nature, but among his hometown folks, "he could do no deed of power there, except that he laid his hands on a few sick people and cured them" (Mark 6:5, NRSV).

The expanding ministry of Jesus is *blocked* and *chained* by the unbelief of his hometown folks and his family. Up to this point, Jesus has provoked amazement and faith in others, but now he is amazed by unbelief.

Jesus had been in the presence of unbelief before he experienced it in his hometown, and in every other situation, he was still able to work many mighty works. In the presence of the unbelief of the scribes, Pharisees, disciples of John the Baptist, and the Herodians, he did many mighty works; but among his own people and their unbelief, his power and influence seem restricted and limited. This refusal of his healing power happens among people who had the strongest and most deeply held opinions about his identity.

Have We Erected Barriers to Jesus' Ministry?

There were three different, strong responses to Jesus' early ministry: 1) The scribes, the Pharisees, and the Herodians reject him completely; 2) the crowds and his disciples believe in him and experience his power; and 3) his hometown folks and family are blinded by their familiarity with him. Isn't it interesting that it is not those who totally reject Jesus who build the strongest barriers to his ministry, but those who know him well? Their knowledge of him, their ideas and definitions of him and who they think he should be, end up creating barriers to fully believing in him. Because they think they know Jesus so well, they end up missing the blessing of his presence and power.

Is it possible that the Church, today's Christians, are like this third group? Have those of us who claim Jesus as our own, who claim to know him best, have doomed and chained ourselves to our doctrines, dogmas, creeds, and cultural translations of who we think he is or should be?

It is very common for people to misunderstand and reject people whom they think they know very well.

National Football Hall of Famer Barry Sanders grew up in Wichita, KS. He started at tailback in his sophomore year of high school, but his younger brother replaced him the following year. He didn't become a starter again until the fourth game of his senior year. Though small in size for a football player, Sanders gained 1,400+ yards in the last seven games of his senior year. Still, he was under-recruited by college football programs. One of the few schools to offer him a scholarship was Oklahoma State University. Sanders took the scholarship and became the backup to another future NFL great, Thurman Thomas. He didn't become a starter at Oklahoma State until his junior year.

That year, he ran for 2,850 yards—an average of 237.5 yards per game—had four, 300-yard games, and scored 44 touchdowns, breaking 34 NCAA records. He won the Heisman Trophy and skipped his senior year of college football. The Detroit Lions drafted him, and, as we like to say, the rest is history.[2]

How did this all-time great player barely play in high school? There were probably many reasons, but for sure, one of the reasons was that the people who knew him first and best were blind to his potential.

You could say that they knew him so well that they couldn't see him. They knew him, defined him, cast him in a role, and placed him in a box that restricted his talent. He won the Heisman Trophy two years later, at Oklahoma State, but his talent didn't appear overnight. It had been there since high school but was blocked by the people who considered themselves experts on Barry Sanders' talent.

What happened to Barry is just like what happened to Jesus among his family and hometown folks, and this is what happens with many Christians today. We think we know Jesus so well, but our proximity to him blinds us from seeing him for who he actually is. We act as if we have exhaustively comprehended and appropriated Jesus with our

2. Kirk, Jason and Kirshner, Alex. "44 Reason Barry Sanders' 1988 is the greatest season in football history." Banner Society, 8 December 2018, https://www.bannersociety.com/2018/12/8/20728939/barry-sanders-1988-college-stats

doctrines, dogmas, creeds, liturgies, and religious experiences, but it is not so. When we act as if we own Jesus and know everything about him, we are in control, not Jesus. Out of such rebellion against his authority, we create idolatrous versions of Jesus to fit our unholy desires and ambitions. We end up putting chains on Jesus' influence in the world.

We cannot fully comprehend Jesus. We don't have the language or mental capacities to understand him fully. He graciously reveals himself to us and within us, and the only proof we have that we have come near him is that his life is *re-presented* through our own. Our lives will be defined by humble service, loving God with our total beings, and loving our neighbors as we love ourselves.

What might be possible for Jesus' impact and influence in the world if we stop trying to own Jesus with our ideas, philosophies, doctrines, dogmas, and cultural representations of him?

As I have spent nearly my entire adult life exploring the person, ministry, and meaning of Jesus, one of my favorite books has been Albert Nolan's brilliant book, *Jesus Before Christianity*.[3] He attempts to get back to the original Jesus of the Gospels before he was *clothed* in the creeds and doctrines of the Church. Whether one agrees with his conclusions or not, what we can value is the attempt to free Jesus' influence and impact from the chains of historical and current interpretations that distort, limit, disfigure, and misrepresent him and, thereby, restrict his influence in the world.

Could the Church be the contemporary hometown and family of Jesus where he is best known but most unwelcome?

Is Jesus welcome in your church?

The Challenge of Free Will

There is at least one other thing to consider if we want to understand how we create restrictions on Jesus' impact upon us.

God created human beings to have free will. In the Garden of Eden, Adam and Eve were free to choose their destiny and were held accountable for the choices they made. The New Testament's concepts of hell and judgment imply that we are free to choose how we will live and will

---

3. Albert Nolan, *Jesus Before Christianity* (Cape Town, South Africa: David Philip Ltd. 1976).

be held accountable for our choices. Although there are centuries-long debates about how much freedom we have, there is general consensus among Christians of all ages that we make choices that determine the quality of our lives.

The biblical witness is clear in the claim that God is omnipotent. However, it is important to acknowledge that, for us to have freewill, God has placed limits on God's power. God doesn't violate the boundaries of our freedom to choose how we will live our lives. God blesses us in ways that guide us toward God's will for us; but, alas, God leaves us with the freedom to choose.

Although our choices cannot and will not thwart God's final and ultimate will, our choices can bring about consequences that impede and frustrate our experience of God's purpose, goodness, and blessings.

Likewise, Jesus is never impotent. Jesus chooses to let us make our choices, and that includes the choices we make about and toward him. He is not different with us than he was with those who came to arrest, charge, imprison, judge, and execute him. The prophecy of Isaiah 53 that Christians apply to Jesus is telling:

> He was oppressed and He was afflicted,
> Yet He opened not His mouth;
> He was led as a lamb to the slaughter,
> And as a sheep before its shearers is silent,
> So, he opened not His mouth.
> (Isaiah 53:7)

When the Roman guards came to arrest him, Jesus didn't object and resist. He submitted to their choice to reject, accuse, and arrest him, although he could have done otherwise. Check out what he said to Pilate at a moment that is on the brink of his execution:

> Then Pilate said to Him, "Are You not speaking to me? Do You not know that I have power to crucify You, and power to release You?"
> Jesus answered, "You could have no power at all against Me unless it had been given you from above." (John 19:10-11)

This same dynamic was at work when Jesus tried to take his ministry to his hometown and to his family. He, for whom all things are possible, could do no great deeds of power there because he would not violate their freedom to choose; and their chosen path was one that rejected Jesus' identity and healing.

All things are still possible for Jesus, but a lack of belief and a lack of surrender to his Lordship and the distortions of him that get created as a result can put restrictions on his power's impact on us. Jesus will heal those who choose and accept his healing grace to be healed.

If we have a *jesus* who loves guns but doesn't love gay people, it is because that is the *jesus* we have created and chosen. If, in our churches, we have a *jesus* who loves prayer vigils in the church chapel but resists praying with prostitutes looking for hope, it is because that is the *jesus* we have created and chosen. If we have a *jesus* who cares about poor children but doesn't care about fetuses, it is because that is the *jesus* we have created and chosen. If we have a *jesus* who cares about what happens to people's souls but doesn't care about what's happening to their bodies, right now, it is because that is the *jesus* we have created and chosen. We could go on and on about how we choose distorted versions of Jesus. None of these versions is even close to being accurate representations of him, but we get to choose, and our choices can become chains around the influence and impact Jesus wants to have on the people in our churches, communities, cities, nations, and world. The *jesus* we experience is the *jesus* we have chosen.

Part of the journey of becoming Jesus' disciples is learning to use our God-given power and freedom of choice to choose to follow, obey, love, and serve Jesus. A mature disciple of Jesus is a person who chooses to let Jesus have unimpeded impact in their life. Indeed, all things are possible when Jesus' desire to bless us meets with our willingness to be blessed by Jesus.

4

THE TOUCHSTONE

"Cut out all the lights. He the Light."

—*Kanye West*[1]

There's a question that begs to be asked at this point in our journey through this book. Given how misinterpretations of Jesus can severely impede Jesus' impact in the world, how do we measure the truthfulness and accuracy of our interpretations of him? It seems like everybody has an opinion about Jesus. Since we know that not all of them help to make Jesus known in the ways that he wants to be known, how do we determine which opinions are valid and which ones are off?

Who's to say that the Ku Klux Klan were wrong in their claim that they were doing the work of Jesus? On what grounds do people reject the prosperity gospel? In chapter 1, I gave a long list of false versions of Jesus. How do we know when a presentation of Jesus is false? Can we move toward some consensus in assessing Christian witness?

One of the reasons that Jesus gets distorted and misrepresented is that Christians, in all places and in all times, must *re-present* Jesus for our different, unique cultures. This work of reinterpreting and *re-presenting* in new and wildly different situations is fraught with the potential for misrepresentation. It is just as ambiguous and delicate a dynamic as the incarnation of God's Word becoming flesh (John 1:1-4). Just as God's incarnation into human flesh was not without misinterpretation and misunderstanding, there is no simple and guaranteed way to bring

1.   Kanye West, "Hands On." *Genius Lyrics*, https://genius.com/Kanye-west-hands-on-lyrics, accessed November 7, 2021.

the Jesus of the Gospels into new contexts without risking distortions of him.

I recently experienced firsthand the difficulty of transferring life from one culture to another when I moved from the urban Southwest of Houston, TX to the rural Midwest of Wichita, KS, with a great deal of arrogance about how effective a pastor I could and would be. I came to Wichita with a lot of presuppositions. My expectations were based on certain identities and labels that I shared with certain groups of people. First, I was a United Methodist pastor going to serve a United Methodist congregation. Next, I was a black pastor going to serve a predominantly black congregation. Furthermore, I was a pastor with experience in serving a very large church going to serve a very large church that wanted a pastor with large-church experience.

With these three primary presuppositions, I began my tenure and headed straight into major conflict on multiple levels, caused mostly by my misreading and misinterpretation of the context. My three presuppositions were, of course, too broad and too general to efficiently aid me in this transfer, to understand the intricacies and details of such a transition.

First while there were certain shared features, United Methodism looked significantly different at Saint Mark's UMC from any of the United Methodist congregations I had served in the Texas Conference. Second, black culture is entirely different in Wichita, Kansas from black culture in the Southwest and, especially, the deep South, where I was born, raised, and lived until the age of twenty-three. Third, while Saint Mark's is a very large church, it is a unique phenomenon in that it did not grow into a very large church the way that I had been taught that churches grow from being a small church into being a very large church or a megachurch. Although it is a large church, it is also very much a family and community church. I came in expecting to lead Saint Mark's with the tools, mindset, and strategies typically used in large megachurches. Think: Explosions!

Conflicts arising from my three major assumptions were just the beginning. There were many other conflicts arising out of clashes of cultures, from dress codes and causal expressions to the significance and role of a pastor in a community and city. One of the major clashes occurred about what it means to "be on time." Coming from Houston, where it takes at least 30–45 minutes to get anywhere, there is a kind of shared agreement, due to the shared awareness of heavy traffic, that if you arrive to a meeting or event 5–10 minutes ahead of time, you're early. If you arrive 2–5 minutes before a meeting, you're on time.

I brought that cultural assumption to Wichita, and it became "a hot mess." In Wichita, you can get from where you are to almost any destination in the city in 18 minutes or less. So, if people make a habit of leaving 30–40 minutes ahead of time to get from one place to another, they regularly arrive at events and meetings early by 15–25 minutes. I went to the city and to Saint Mark's determined to be on time for every meeting and every event, which, in my mind, meant right on time or 2–3 minutes before the meeting was to begin. After a few months, an elderly truthteller in Saint Mark's affectionately known as "Brother Eugene" took me to lunch to "get to know me;" as we were ending the lunch, he included in his parting words of guidance, ". . . and stop being late for everything!"

His comment startled me. "Late?" I thought to myself. I had been determined to be on time for everything. Later that day, as I reflected on that conversation, I started reviewing people's reactions and interactions to me at various meetings and events, and "my eyes came open." What I had been interpreting as people being closed and unwelcoming to a newcomer was actually irritation at my consistently getting to meetings "right on time." When I adjusted my arrival time for meetings and events, I started to feel more welcome and embraced by the culture and the people. Something that simple, a difference in cultural practices, was causing misinterpretations, misunderstandings, and conflict.

If a guy from the Southwest and a community of people in the rural Midwest have cultural differences that create significant conflicts, then it is no surprise that we encounter all kinds of conflicts when we try to *re-present* Jesus of Nazareth in our twenty-first-century contexts and cultures. Think: "Explosions!"

Furthermore, consider the additional conflicts that occur when two different cultures compare reinterpretations and representations of Jesus. How Jesus looks in a village in Nigeria will be quite different from how Jesus is represented in a wealthy, predominantly white suburb of Chicago, IL. It's the same Jesus, but he will *look* quite different in those two contexts.

This is, in part, how we end up with so many distortions, perversions, misinterpretations, and misrepresentations of Jesus. Translating

Jesus and his story into new cultural and historical contexts is difficult work, fraught with innumerable dangers and pitfalls.

I think it is possible that this is the reason for Jesus saying, "Shhhh—keep quiet about me" (referred to as the "messianic secret) in the aftermath of some of the miracles that he worked. This may have been Jesus' acknowledgment that, even in his own time, the work of translating his person, teachings, and ministry to new audiences and new contexts was riddled with potential for distortion and misrepresentation (see Mark 1:34, 40-45; 3:11-12; 5:43). Even in his own day, Jesus was wary of some interpretations of him. He was particularly opposed to demons talking about him. Nothing can cause distortions of Jesus more than supernatural knowledge combined with agendas that are radically opposed to Jesus' life and mission.

When we engage in the work of lifting up Jesus without care, caution, and prudence, not only do we cause "cultural explosions"; we eventually end up distorting Jesus so profoundly that he is no longer the Jesus of Scripture but a creature of our own making. How can we improve our chances of avoiding this fate? Is there a way of doing the work of reinterpreting and *re-presenting* Jesus that increases the likelihood that that people can better experience him and cultivate a relationship with him?

Yes. We can do the work of reinterpreting and *re-presenting* Jesus effectively and productively if we are relentlessly committed to the central claim of the Christian Faith: Jesus Christ is Lord. When those of us who claim Jesus as Lord and confess to follow him don't really think, believe, and live by this central claim, we create distorted presentations of Jesus that do great harm.

But what does "Jesus Christ is Lord" really mean?

In an article with the title, "Lord," theologian Ben Witherington III explains how that title was used in Jesus' culture and context. The title, *Lord* (Greek: *kyrios*), could refer to "a deity who can answer prayers and deserves thanks for divine help." It was also a title used to refer to the Roman Emperor. *Lord* was used by early Christian communities (especially those with some connection to the apostle Paul) to refer to "an absolute divine being to whom one belongs and owes absolute allegiance and submission." For Jews in Jesus' context, *Lord* was a name and title to be used, specifically and uniquely, for God.[2] All the above

---

2. Ben Witherington III, "Lord," in *Dictionary of Jesus and the Gospels*, 2nd Edition Joel B. Green, Jeannine K. Brown, and Nicholas Perrin, editors (Downers

usages seemed to have been adapted by early Christians and transferred to Jesus.

It is worth noting that the comprehensive New Testament view of the Lordship of Jesus isn't grounded in his divinity alone. There is a clear assertion among some New Testament writers that his Lordship is grounded in his earthly life of obedience as a human being to the will of God. In the Acts of the Apostles, the writer has Peter preaching the first sermon after the resurrection of Jesus and the coming of the Holy Spirit. Peter gives testimony to Jesus, and says to his listeners:

> Jesus of Nazareth, a Man attested by God to you by miracles, wonders, and signs which God did through Him in your midst, as you yourselves also know—Him, being delivered by the determined purpose and foreknowledge of God, you have taken by lawless hands, have crucified, and put to death; whom God raised up, having loosed the pains of death, because it was not possible that He should be held by it. . . .

"Therefore, let all the house of Israel know assuredly that God has *made* this Jesus, whom you crucified, both Lord and Christ." (Acts 2:22-24, 36; italics added).

And then there's the great passage in Philippians 2:5-11, where Paul implies that the Lordship of Jesus was not present in the beginning but was determined by God in response to Jesus' faithful obedience, even to the point of death:

> Let this mind be in you which was also in Christ Jesus, who, being in the form of God, did not consider it robbery to be equal with God, but made Himself of no reputation, taking the form of a bondservant, and coming in the likeness of men. And being found in appearance as a man, He humbled Himself and became obedient to THE POINT OF death, even the death of the cross. Therefore, God also has highly exalted Him and given Him the name which is above every name, that at the name of Jesus every knee should bow, of those in heaven, and of those on earth, and of those under the earth, and that every tongue should confess that Jesus Christ is Lord, to the glory of God the Father.

The point here is that, when we confess Jesus as Lord, we must include *both* the supernatural presence of Jesus in our hearts and the earthly Jesus who walked the roads of the Fertile Crescent. If we limit

Grove, IL: InterVarsity Press, 2013), 526.

Jesus' Lordship to the supernatural Jesus in our hearts, his Lordship will become ethereal, otherworldly, and immeasurable.

It is irrational and dangerous to claim Jesus as Lord but then act as if he can be known only as a presence in our personal hearts. Our personal hearts are too wicked to be the only measure of an authentic experience of Jesus. "The heart is devious above all else; / it is perverse— / who can understand it?" (Jeremiah17:9, NRSV). Of course, his spiritual Lordship is powerful and effective, but in order to guard the integrity of this personal relationship we have with Jesus, we must measure this relationship by how Jesus lived, in the flesh, while on earth. We can know he has spoken to us when the words we heard in our heart are consistent with his earthly words and deeds as recorded in the Gospels. Beware of versions of Jesus that come solely from the heart of a human being.

Grounding and embracing Jesus' Lordship of our lives in both his earthly and supernatural life is more consistent with the comprehensive view found in the New Testament, and it meets our need for a spirituality that's both transcendent and measurable.

As we embrace the Lordship of Jesus, fully, in all its dimensions, Jesus becomes the measure, the touchstone, by which we examine, assess, guide, correct, and, if necessary, reject claims about Jesus, the Christian faith, and Christian practice. Jesus becomes our measure of everything!

We will measure our use of resources by Jesus. We will measure our marriages by Jesus. We will measure our politics by Jesus. We will measure our opinions, worldviews, philosophies, and theologies by Jesus. We will measure our expressions of church and ministry by Jesus. We will measure our budgets and our investments by Jesus. We will measure our passions and desires by Jesus.

The Lordship of Jesus will be the filter through which we will process our disagreements of who Jesus is for our culture and times. We will work through the differences in our cultural *re-presentations* of Jesus by placing all things "on the altar" of the Light of the world. This doesn't mean that we will suddenly agree on everything, but we will at least know how to have more fruitful battles that lead to more faithful discipleship among all of us because how we disagree will also be guided by Jesus our Lord and Savior.

When we take seriously the Lordship of Jesus, we will do what the author of the epistle to the Hebrews encourages us to do: "Keep your eyes on *Jesus*, who both began and finished this race we're in. Study how he did it. Because he never lost sight of where he was headed—that exhilarating finish in and with God—he could put up with anything along the way: Cross, shame, whatever. And now he's *there*, in the place of honor, right alongside God" (Hebrews 12:2, MSG; italics original).

Why should we measure our commitment to Jesus at all? We measure because, if Jesus is our Lord, our greatest desire is to obey and please him; we measure by Jesus because Jesus told us that he is "the way, the truth, the life" (John 14:6). We measure by Jesus because the collective claim of the New Testament is that the goal of becoming Jesus' disciples is to become like him. In one place, Paul says that the ultimate good of life is to be conformed to the "image" of Jesus (Romans 8:29). In another place, Paul (or a protégé of Paul) tells us that the ultimate consummation of the body of Christ—the fellowship of all believers—is that we "come to the unity of the faith and of the knowledge of the Son of God, to maturity, to the measure of the full stature of Christ" (Ephesians 4:13, NRSV).

One of my favorite preachers of all time, the late Dr. Gardner C. Taylor, once said in a sermon that our goal is to become so much like Jesus that, when we stand before God in final judgment with Jesus the advocate at our side, God will look at the two of us and ask, "Which one is Jesus?"

I would add just one little adjustment to Dr. Taylor's analogy. The vision given to us by the writer of Ephesians is clear that no one of us alone can become the "measure of the full stature of Christ." We become like Jesus, together.

5
ORGANIC JESUS

Taken out of context I must seem so strange.

—Ani DiFranco, American singer-songwriter[1]

We impede the impact of Jesus when we disconnect him from the faith and heritage into which he was born and fully embraced, the faith that he died seeking to fulfill.

Furthermore, if we disconnect Jesus from who he was, then we can make him mean anything and everything, and if he means anything and everything, then he will mean nothing . . . at least not something that really matters.

One of the first things I learned about studying and interpreting the Bible is to distinguish between what a biblical passage meant and what it means. When we are interpreting any literature, we are looking for meaning for ourselves in the present moment, and we can make a written text mean anything we want it to mean for us. However, for some of us, and I certainly hope that this is true of you, what a text means for *us* has to be connected to what it meant coming from the original authors and editors. For some of us, it is dishonest and *slippery* to claim to value what someone else wrote or said without any sincere regard for what the person meant, twisting their words for our own purposes and agendas. What we determine their words to mean for us has to be connected to what the authors or writers meant.

Honoring the original meaning of words should be of even greater importance when we approach the sacred texts, the foundation upon

---

1. Ani DiFranco, "Fire Door," *Ani DiFranco,* © Righteous Babe Records, 1990.

which our shared faith is built. My preaching professor, Dr. Zan W. Holmes used to tell his students to "wrestle with and be faithful to the text." He strongly encouraged us to let our application of a text be guided by the original meaning of the text as best as we could determine.

If we are going to try to *re-present* Jesus for our times and contexts, we should begin with the work of trying to understand what his life meant and what the stories about him meant. We can even ask, "What was, and is, God saying to us by choosing this particular context as the circumstance through which to communicate the 'Word made flesh'?"

This is, indeed, an extraordinarily challenging task; to do it well, we have to work our way through many layers of experiences, witness, writings, sermons, traditions, doctrines, and stories of and about Jesus, go to the Gospels, and then try to catch at least a glimpse of the actual Jesus about whom the Gospels bear witness. We must relentlessly explore what the Gospels meant to their first readers. We must explore what Jesus meant. We must explore what God meant by sending Jesus through a specific historical context. Maybe then, we can explore what these things can mean for us today.

I know this isn't how some people choose to approach Jesus. For many people and many Christians, the Jesus who lived as a human being on earth in a particular time and context doesn't matter. For these persons, all that matters is who Jesus is to them personally in their individual hearts. In fact, the apostle Paul, to a great degree, doesn't give much attention to the life of Jesus (which is the reason, by the way, that many New Testament scholars say that Paul was the actual creator of the new religion called *Christianity*).

Also, there are persons who have no attention for and place no value in the Jesus who lived on earth, because the only Jesus they know or care to know, is the Jesus who has been passed on to us through dogma, creeds, theological formulas, liturgies, icons, ceremonies, experiences, traditions, and religious movements. For these people, the only Jesus who matters is a *spiritual* (as distinct from physical or tangible) Jesus that we worship and explore, theologically, as a supernatural reality. In many cases, the more the Church worships him, and the more we theologize about him, the less interest we have in the life he actually lived. The more he becomes the Christ of our creeds, the less we care about him as Jesus the Palestinian Jew.

However, if Jesus is completely otherworldly, ethereal, celestial, metaphysical, intangible, transcendent, and undefinable, then we can make him mean whatever we want him to mean. To a great degree, that's exactly what we have done.

I take seriously the earthly, tangible life of Jesus. I assume that who Jesus is today and who he was in the first century are one reality. I assume that the only way to assess the validity of claims about personal and spiritual experiences of Jesus is to place them in the light of who he was and how he lived as a first-century, Palestinian Israelite. We must visit Jesus in his original context, the setting in which God decided to place Jesus as God's most decisive and most significant speech to us (Hebrews 1:1-2). Jesus' cultural moment is not incidental. According to Jesus, it was chosen by God as the right and ripe context in which and from which God would communicate God's most important message. As we "paint a picture" of Jesus in the chapters ahead, that picture will be shaped by the context in which Jesus lived.

A First-Century Palestinian Israelite

I want to lay out some details about Jesus that are loaded with meaning and contain numerous implications. However, I want to be clear about my objectives. First, I am not attempting to do a "search for the historical Jesus," although I greatly appreciate the work that has been by scholars on this matter. Second, I am not trying to make an argument about the depth of Jesus' Jewishness. My objective is to take seriously the information we are given about Jesus in the Gospels and connect Jesus and that information to their historical contexts. Third, while I am aware that each of the Gospels has its own authorship, audience, date of writing, and social context, I focus more on the collective picture they give us of Jesus. The fact that there are differences in the details of their narratives about Jesus does not diminish the fact that, together, they give us a holistic picture of Jesus.

I want to begin with Rabbi Joseph Telushkin's assessment of the picture of Jesus as given in the Gospels. "The New Testament depiction of Jesus suggests that he was largely a law-abiding and highly nationalistic Jew, and a man with strong ethical concerns. Like many of Judaism's great rabbis, he saw love of neighbor as religion's central demand. Though many Christians are under the impression that he opposed Judaism's emphasis on law, in actuality he criticized anyone who advocated dropping it."[2] Telushkin goes on to say that, while Jewish scholars differ widely in their understanding of who Jesus was, "almost no Jewish scholars believe that Jesus intended to start a new religion. Were Jesus to return today, most Jews believe, he undoubtedly would feel more at home in a synagogue than a church."[3] The Gospels present the life of someone who was born an Israelite, lived as a Israelite, viewed the world as an Israelite, and died as an Israelite.

Jesus was born an Israelite. The term *Jew* didn't arise until the fourth century, around 6–4 BC in the town of Bethlehem. His name in Hebrew is *Yeshua*, a common male name of Jesus' time, derived from *Yehoshua* (Joshua), which means "to rescue" or "to deliver." Joseph is told by an angel to give him this name because "He will save His people from their sins" (Matthew 1:21). His mother and the man to whom she was engaged to be married, Joseph, were from either Bethlehem (Matthew 2:22-23) or Nazareth (Luke 2:1-7). After Jesus' birth, the significance of which was revealed to multiple persons by divine revelation (Matthew 1–2; Luke 1–2), Mary and Joseph had Jesus circumcised on the eighth day, in alignment with Israelite law and custom.

Matthew (2:13-15) tells us that after Jesus' circumcision, Mary and Joseph fled to Egypt for a period to protect Jesus from Herod the Great's genocide of Bethlehem's babies from the age of two and under. The family returned and eventually settled in Nazareth where Jesus lived and grew into adulthood. We are not told much else about Jesus' life after his family settled in Nazareth, except a few details, all from Luke:

– As he settled with his family in Nazareth, Jesus "grew and became strong in spirit, filled with wisdom; and the grace of God was upon Him" (Luke 2:40);

– Mary and Joseph were devout Israelites who made the trek to Jerusalem every year for the Passover Feast. At age twelve, Jesus made the journey with them and was left behind; Mary and Joseph found him in the Temple, "sitting in the

---

2. Joseph Telushkin, *Jewish Literacy*, (Harper Collins, 1991), 123.
3. Telushkin, *Jewish Literacy*, 123–24.

midst of the teachers, both listening to them and asking them questions" (Luke 2:46);

- By the age of twelve, Jesus was already developing an extraordinary sense of calling and mission and an intense, unique relationship with God (Luke 2:47-49);

- Until he showed up at the Jordan River to be baptized by his cousin, John the Baptist, Jesus subjected himself to his parents' authority (Luke 2:51).

We also learn that, until Jesus began his public ministry, he worked with Joseph as a carpenter (Mark 6:3; Matthew 13:54-55).

Throughout his life, as attested to in the Gospels, Jesus is deeply rooted in the life, rituals, and practices of first-century Israelite faith. He worships in the synagogues. He preaches from Israel's Scriptures (Luke 4:16-20). He demonstrates respect for Israelite customs and laws (Luke 5:14; 17:14). He interprets life and events through the lens of Scripture, including within some of the most crucial moments and conversations of his life: when he faces temptation (Matthew 4:1-11), when he defines the most important commandment (Matthew 22:37-40), when he interprets the ministry of John the Baptist in relation to his own (Matthew 11:10; Luke 7:27), when he acts against what he sees as abuse in the Temple (Matthew 21:13; Mark 11:17; Luke 19:46), and even when on the cross (Matthew 27:46; Mark 15:34).

All these details converge to give us a picture of a Jesus who was, through and through, a person deeply rooted in the life and traditions of first-century, Israelite faith. There are some broader dimensions to first-century Israelite faith that, while not explicitly stated in the Gospels, are implied and present in the mind of Jesus as we see him in public life. I mention them briefly, but we will visit them in more detail later as we see how they were lived out in the story of Jesus.

A God-Centered View of Reality

The Israelites were not unique because they believed in God. Belief in divine beings was common in the ancient world. The first-century Mediterranean world, ruled by the Roman empire, was filled with gods and temples in which to worship and make sacrifices. There was a god for every human concern. There was also the imperial religion of the Romans, defined by worship and sacrifices to the Roman emperor. The Roman, Hellenistic attitude toward religion was that as long as you made appropriate sacrifices to the emperor, you were free to have as many gods and temples as you wanted.

So it wasn't that they believed in God that made the Israelites unique and different. It was how they believed in God that distinguished them. In the religious syncretism of the times, Jesus and all first-century Israelites were distinguished by their *monotheism*, that is, belief in one God. In the words of the apostle Paul, "yet for us there is one God, the Father, from whom are all things and for whom we exist" (1 Corinthians 8:6, NRSV). In another biblical passage, found in the Acts of the Apostles, we are told of a story in which Paul is in Athens (think Greek religious syncretism), disturbed by what he views as alarming idolatry displayed by the worship of many gods. Some Epicurean and Stoic philosophers take him to the Areopagus to speak about the faith that he has been proclaiming in Athens. There, Paul sees an inscription to "the Unknown God," and what he says in response is a direct reflection of Israelite monotheism.

> Men of Athens, I perceive that in all things you are very religious; for as I was passing through and considering the objects of your worship, I even found an altar with this inscription:
>
> *TO THE UNKNOWN GOD.*
>
> Therefore, the One whom you worship without knowing, Him I proclaim to you: God, who made the world and everything in it, since He is Lord of heaven and earth, does not dwell in temples made with hands. Nor is He worshiped with men's hands, as though He needed anything, since He gives to all life, breath, and all things. And He has made from one blood every nation of men to dwell on all the face of the earth, and has determined their pre-appointed times and the boundaries of their dwellings, so that they should seek the Lord, in the hope that they might grope for Him and find Him, though He is not far from each one of us; for in Him we live and move and have our being (Acts 17:22-28a).

Paul, of course, broke from his fellow Israelites in how he saw and interpreted Jesus. Nevertheless, his emphasis on one God by whom all things exist is a completely Israelite assertion.

Paul, Jesus, and the Israelites of the first century were well-rooted in the core belief of Israelite faith, encoded in the first statement of what is called the *Shema*. Rabbi Joseph Telushkin explains,

> Although Judaism has no catechism, the biblical verse "sh'ma Yisra'el, Adonai Eloheinu, Adonai Ekhad—Hear, O Israel, the Lord Is Our God, the Lord Is One" (Deuteronomy 6:4), comes closest to being Judaism's credo. In just six Hebrew words, it sums up Judaism's belief in monotheism, and its rejection of all idols. For two thousand years, the Sh'ma has been the verse with which many Jewish martyrs have gone to their deaths, while those fortunate enough to meet more peaceful endings try to die with the Sh'ma on their lips. To this day, Jews are supposed to recite the Sh'ma four times a day, twice during morning prayers, once during the evening service, and, finally, at home before going to sleep.[4]

Following the *Shema* is what is called the *V'ahavta*: "You shall love the LORD your God with all your heart, with all your soul, and with all your strength" (Deuteronomy 6:5). Together, the *Shema* and the *V'ahavta* assert the core of Israelite faith that there is one God, who is King and Lord of all, and who is to be given singular obedience, loyalty, and worship. This is why there is such a relentless stance against idolatry through the Hebrew Bible (and in the New Testament, as well). Combined with these core beliefs is the belief that this one God, the Lord of all reality, had chosen to enter into covenant relationship with Israel, beginning with Abraham. Fidelity to their covenant relationship with this God was/is a matter of life and death. It is important to understand that most Jews interpret their history, including their history as reported in the Hebrew Bible, through the lens of these core beliefs.

These core beliefs set the Israelites apart in the world under Roman rule and were so tightly held that the Roman empire made exceptions, in many cases, to try to prevent conflict with Israelite communities.[5]

Further, the Israelites viewed God as the center of all life, not just religious life. In the cultural religions of the Roman/Hellenistic first century, gods were viewed as useful for certain things. While there was a god for every human need, there was no loyalty beyond a god's usefulness. For the Israelites, however, everything was spiritual. There was no separation of sacred and secular. There was no separation of religious

---

4. Telushkin, *Jewish Literacy*, Revised Ed, 746, Kindle.

5. E.P. Sanders, "Jesus: Jewish Palestine at the Time of Jesus," *Britannica*, https://www.britannica.com/biography/Jesus/Jewish-Palestine-at-the-time-of-Jesus.

practice and ordinary life. The Torah and the Divine covenant included all dimensions of life. God was at the center of everything.

These core Israelite beliefs constituted the core of Jesus' faith. He fully embraced them. They shaped his worldview. They determined his actions. And they were so deeply held by his fellow Israelites that they were, in part, the beliefs that led to his execution.

Divine Intervention

The Israelites believed in divine intervention within human affairs. While this belief was not unique to them, it was essential to their faith. In fact, Israelite faith originated in an act of divine intervention: God's deliverance of the Israelites out of Egyptian slavery. This act of deliverance is the basis upon which God called the newly liberated Israelites into covenant relationship.

> When your children ask you in time to come, "What is the meaning of the decrees and the statutes and the ordinances that the LORD our God has commanded you?" then you shall say to your children, "We were Pharaoh's slaves in Egypt, but the LORD brought us out of Egypt with a mighty hand. The LORD displayed before our eyes great and awesome signs and wonders against Egypt, against Pharaoh and all his household. He brought us out from there in order to bring us in, to give us the land that he promised on oath to our ancestors. Then the LORD commanded us to observe all these statutes, to fear the LORD our God, for our lasting good, so as to keep us alive, as is now the case. If we diligently observe this entire commandment before the LORD our God, as he has commanded us, we will be in the right." (Deuteronomy 6:20-25, NRSV)

Given how their covenant relationship with God begins with God's direct intervention into their circumstances, it is no surprise that the Israelites viewed the world as a realm in which God not only intervened but did so regularly. New Testament scholar E. P. Sanders says that, along with the official leaders of Israelite faith in the first century—the Pharisees, the Sadducees, the scribes, the priests, and the Levites—Palestine had "charismatic healers and miracle workers, such as Honi the Circle Drawer and Hanina ben Dosa; hermitlike sages, such as Bannus; eschatological prophets, such as John the Baptist; would-be messianic prophets, such as Theudas the Egyptian; and apocalyptic visionaries."[6] In fact, the idea of a god who exists but is uninvolved in human affairs was not significant until the rise of deism in sixteenth-century France.

The expectation of continued divine intervention was the womb in which the Israelites nurtured their expectation of a messiah-figure who would come to restore Israel and lead them to fulfill their promised destiny.

From the picture of Jesus presented collectively in the Gospels, Jesus fully believed in God's constant intervention in human affairs, and he was fully aware of the expectation that this intervention would eventually come through a messiah. In whatever sense Jesus saw himself as the expected messiah, he saw himself as the vehicle for a decisive divine intervention in the life of Israel and human history.

Community as Identity, Identity in Community

As from the beginning of Israelite faith, the self-identity of the Israelites of the first century was defined by communal consciousness. Reality, truth, life, and goodness were defined by and experienced in community with others. While there was certainly a cultivation of individual responsibility, the goal of individual responsibility was to help the community of God's chosen people to do well and flourish.

This self-understanding as community is radically different from the perspective of Christians in our times, especially in North America. Often, we read the Bible through the lens of relentless individualism, a core value of American society. In so doing, we greatly miss and distort the messages and meanings of Scripture. The Israelites, Jesus, the early Christians, the Torah, and the New Testament: none of these present an individualistic understanding of life.

In the Israelite creation story, even God, in God's first self-reference, uses communal language. "Let *us* make humankind" (Genesis 1:26, NRSV, italics added). God's covenant is with the community of Israelites. Throughout the Torah and Hebrew Scriptures, individual behavior

6. E.P. Sanders, "Jesus: The Jewish Religion in the 1st Century," *Britannica*, https://www.britannica.com/biography/Jesus/The-Jewish-religion-in-the-1st-century.

is given great weight only because of its impact upon the community. Sins travel throughout the community and into ensuing generations. The Israelites are God's chosen people so that they, as a community, can be used by God to bless the community of all people (Genesis 12:1-4). When Jesus comes, the good news he announces is about a new kind of community, the Kingdom of God (Mark 1:14-15).

We simply cannot understand Jesus as he wants us to understand him unless we understand him as one who is radically oriented toward community. When Jesus launched his ministry, his mission and vision were about building a certain kind of community.

A Missional People

Since the beginning of God's covenant with the Israelites, they saw themselves as a missional people. *Missional* is not, of course, a term that they would have used. It is a modern word, but it captures the idea of *existing for the sake of serving others.* The initiation of the Abrahamic covenant was thought of as the Israelites' special relationship with God. Abraham and all his descendants were, to use a contemporary phrase, "blessed to be a blessing." Notice how it is worded in the story of Abraham's calling:

> Now the LORD said to Abram, "Go from your country and your kindred and your father's house to the land that I will show you. I will make of you a great nation, and I will bless you, and make your name great, so that you will be a blessing. I will bless those who bless you, and the one who curses you I will curse; and in you all the families of the earth shall be blessed." (Genesis 12:1-4, NRSV)

Christopher Wright points out that, not only did the Israelites see themselves as a missional people, but they believed that "God himself has a mission. God has a purpose and goal for his whole creation."[7]

This pillar of Israel's self-understanding is at work in the life of Jesus as we see it in the Gospels. Jesus expresses a sense of special calling and uniqueness, that of serving the world. Jesus lives his life on a mission. He calls others to share this mission of being a blessing to the world. When he sends his followers out, he is sending them out to be a blessing

---

7.   Christopher Wright, *The Mission of God's People,* (Grand Rapids, MI: Zondervan, 2010), 24.

to others (Matthew 4:19; 10; 28:16-20; Mark 16:14-18; John 20:19-23).

Any attempt at following Jesus, understanding, or representing Jesus—his faith, his life, and his mission—that doesn't have at its core a fundamental sense of being called to go and serve others is a profound distortion of the One who declares that he came to "to seek and to save that which was lost" (Luke 19:10).

A Faith Built on a Story of Deliverance

Along with the covenant established with them through Abraham, the Israelites understood themselves as people whom God delivered out of Egyptian slavery and into the land of Canaan. If the covenant established with Abraham brought them into a relationship of special blessedness, their deliverance gave them the motivation to be faithful to their covenant with God. The deliverance from Egypt was the basis for God's command to live a life of communal obedience and faithfulness. It was the basis for God's command to reject idols. It was the basis for their confidence in God's future provision.

God had instructed Moses, at the burning bush in the Midian desert, to go and deliver the Israelites from Egyptian slavery and bring them to Mount Sinai to worship God. In Exodus 20, the deliverance is fulfilled; their enemies have drowned in the Red Sea by God's hands. They are at the foot of Mount Sinai, about to receive God's Law, their *map* as a newly liberated people who have now been given the responsibility of self-determination. They know about Yahweh. They know that they are in covenant with God. Yet, this is the first time they will hear from God, through Moses, directly as a gathered community. Mount Sinai is in the embrace of God's presence. There is fire, then smoke, and then earthquakes. Then, there is the sound of Israel's trumpet, growing louder and louder. Then God reveals God's identity to set the stage for the people to hear and be obligated to God's instructions. After all of this, what are the first words from God? What is the big reveal?

At Sinai, God doesn't use the same self-identifying *label* that was used with Moses in the Midian desert:

Moreover God said to Moses, "Thus you shall say to the children of Israel:

45

'The LORD God of your fathers, the God of Abraham, the God of Isaac, and the God of Jacob, has sent me to you. This IS My name forever, and this is My memorial to all generations.'" (Exodus 3:15, NRSV)

The *label* that Moses was to give the Israelites in Egypt is this:

"I am the LORD your God, who brought you out of the land of Egypt, out of the house of slavery." (Exodus 20:2, NRSV)

This self-identifying phrase becomes the foundation for the Israelites to gather as an organized, self-determining, nation-building people. This is how the Israelites defined themselves from this point onward. This was the story that became the constant reminder and call to them to be faithful to the covenant established through Abraham. Every time they were in trouble from threats from surrounding nations, it was this story that gave them confidence to face their enemies in battle. When the Northern Kingdom of Israel and the Southern Kingdom of Judah were sacked and God's people carried off into captivity, it was this story of liberation, this sacred memory, that became their hope for future restoration.

One of the most passionate references to this is found in Deuteronomy, the story of God's words of caution to the Israelites as they were preparing to enter the land of promise:

Hear, O Israel: The LORD is our God, the LORD alone. You shall love the LORD your God with all your heart, and with all your soul, and with all your might. Keep these words that I am commanding you today in your heart. Recite them to your children and talk about them when you are at home and when you are away, when you lie down and when you rise. Bind them as a sign on your hand, fix them as an emblem on your forehead, and write them on the doorposts of your house and on your gates.

When the LORD your God has brought you into the land that he swore to your ancestors, to Abraham, to Isaac, and to Jacob, to give you— a land with fine, large cities that you did not build, houses filled with all sorts of goods that you did not fill, hewn cisterns that you did not hew, vineyards and olive groves that you did not plant—and when you have eaten your fill, take care that you do not forget the LORD, who brought you out of the land of Egypt, out of the house of slavery. The LORD your God you shall fear; him you shall serve, and by his name alone you shall swear. Do not follow other gods, any of the gods of the peoples who are all around you, because the LORD your God, who is present with you, is a jealous God. The anger of the LORD your God would be kindled against you and he would destroy you from the face of the earth.

Do not put the LORD your God to the test, as you tested him at Massah. You must diligently keep the commandments of the LORD your God, and his decrees, and his statutes that he has commanded you. Do what is right and good in the sight of the LORD, so that it may go well with you, and so that you may go in and occupy the good land that the LORD swore to your ancestors to give you, thrusting out all your enemies from before you, as the LORD has promised.

When your children ask you in time to come, "What is the meaning of the decrees and the statutes and the ordinances that the LORD our God has commanded you?" then you shall say to your children, "We were Pharaoh's slaves in Egypt, but the LORD brought us out of Egypt with a mighty hand. The LORD displayed before our eyes great and awesome signs and wonders against Egypt, against Pharaoh and all his household. He brought us out from there in order to bring us in, to give us the land that he promised on oath to our ancestors. Then the LORD commanded us to observe all these statutes, to fear the LORD our God, for our lasting good, so as to keep us alive, as is now the case. If we diligently observe this entire commandment before the LORD our God, as he has commanded us, we will be in the right. (Deuteronomy 6:4-25, NRSV)

The promise and the covenant made with the Israelites through Abraham was important and fundamental, but it was validated and proved in God's mighty deliverance of the Israelites from slavery in Egypt.

If this is the faith that Jesus inherited, embraced, lived by, and died for, and if this is the founding story that shaped his self-identity and how he understood his mission, then we can't rightfully speak of Jesus as having nothing to do with our social, political, and economic circumstances. It was not a spiritual deliverance that formed their identity. It was deliverance from an actual situation of social oppression. This doesn't mean that Jesus and his fellow Israelites were "liberation theologians," whatever we mean by that label. It does, however, mean that, as followers of Jesus, we can't restrict Christian thought and practice to individual, spiritual matters. The Israelites viewed God as the center of all of life, not just religious life; and God cares about everything in our lives. To use a phrase often used by a popular spiritual teacher and is the title of one of his books, "everything is spiritual."[8]

When talking about recognizing the true Jesus, Jesus the Israelite, we need to pay attention to how the Israelites and Jesus talked about God and lived out their religious faith and practice. When the Israelites wanted to teach about the nature of God or describe the nature of authentic faith, they told stories, as opposed to engaging in abstract thinking. Who is God to an Israelite? *God is the One who freed us from the land of Egypt, where we were slaves.* It is, then, no surprise that, when Jesus engages in the ministry of teaching, he constantly uses stories and experiences to explain faith and point people to God.

In the history of the Church, Jesus has often been defined for the world by Greek ideas, philosophical ruminations, theological abstractions, and academic speculations. There is certainly value for us in these exercises. The psalm-derived phrase, "let everything praise the LORD!" (Psalm 150), comes to mind. Without doubt, many of the efforts of these intellectual investigations of divine truth have been helpful contributions to our discernment about Jesus and divine realities.

However, if these contributions become our only definitive statements and doctrines of faith, we place devastating misunderstandings on Jesus' impact in the world. Jesus came from a people who used stories to speak of truth and the divine. Jesus himself comes to us as a story. Telling stories about Jesus is fundamental to our Christian witness.

I once heard a very interesting story about Thomas Aquinas, the renowned theologian of the Middle Ages who wrote volumes of books on theology, including the highly influential, *Summa Theologica.* Supposedly, while on his death bed, he had an experience of the presence of God; afterward, he declared that everything he had written was wrong. Then he took his last breath. I have not been able to verify this story, but I like it because it speaks so powerfully to the nature of Jewish and Christian faith. There is, no doubt, great value in Aquinas's theological offerings, but this story of his experience of God, if true, took prominence for him in his last moments.

8.   Rob Bell, *Everything is Spiritual: A Brief Guide to Who We Are and What We're Doing Here,* (New York, NY: St. Martin's Press, 2021).

A Surprise Twist?

While most first-century Israelites were not a part of a sect or sub-group within the Israelite faith, four primary groups shaped the political thinking and action of the period: the Essenes, the Sadducees, the Pharisees, and the Zealots.

The Essenes were committed to communal living, an ascetic lifestyle, and a rigorous religious discipline. They were like the monastic communities that we know of in our time, except that they didn't fully separate themselves from the broader communities in which they lived. They rejected personal wealth and engaged in communal sharing of goods in a way that's very similar to the what is described in Acts (2:43-47; 4:32-37). They leaned toward rejection of secular culture. Some scholars suggest that the Qumran community, from whom we get the Dead Sea scrolls, were an Essene community, one that became totally disillusioned with society-at-large and Temple-focused Israelite life in particular. The first-century historian Josephus, who is one of the few sources we have for descriptions of Israelite faith of the time, gives us this very interesting observation about the Essenes: "there are also among them those who profess to foretell what is to come, being thoroughly trained in holy books, various purifications, and concise sayings of prophets. Rarely if ever do they fail in their predictions."[9]

The Sadducees were aristocratic Israelites, including high priests and merchants, who managed the affairs of the Temple, political relationships, the collection of taxes, the Israelite military, and the relationship between the Israelites and the Roman prefect. For the Sadducees, only the written laws of the Torah were authoritative, and they gave very little, if any at all, credence to the oral teachings on the Torah that were popular among scribes and Pharisees. They "came close to being biblical literalists."[10] Kaufmann Kohler notes the polemic that happens between Jesus and the Sadducees in the Gospels:

> Representing the nobility, power, and wealth, they had centered their interests in political life, of which they were the chief rulers. Instead of sharing the Messianic hopes of the Pharisees, who committed the future into the hand of God, they took the people's destiny into their own hands,

---

9. Steve Mason, "Judean War," *Flavius Josephus: Translation and Commentary*, vol. 1b (Leiden: Brill, 2008), 128.
10. Telushkin, *Jewish Literacy*, 130.

fighting or negotiating with the heathen nations just as they thought best, while having as their aim their own temporary welfare and worldly success. This is the meaning of what Josephus chooses to term their disbelief in fate and divine providence. . . .

As the logical consequence of the preceding view, they would not accept the Pharisaic doctrine of the resurrection, which was a national rather than an individual hope. As to the immortality of the soul, they seem to have denied this as well. . . .

According to Jesephus, they regarded only those observances as obligatory which are contained in the written word, and did not recognize those not written in the law of Moses and declared by the Pharisees to be derived from the traditions of the fathers. Instead of accepting the authority of the teachers, they considered it a virtue to dispute it by arguments. . . .

According to Acts xxiii. 8, they denied also the existence of angels and demons.[11]

Because they were so completely tied to the Temple, the Sadducees ceased to exist after the final destruction of the Temple in AD 70. They left no writings, so most of what we know about them came from the group who were their political and intra-faith rivals, the Pharisees.

The Pharisees, in contrast to the Sadducees, embraced the oral teachings on the Torah that came from the scribes (teachers of the Torah and Mosaic Law), and received and passed on those oral teachings as authoritative for Israelite faith. Additionally, they differed from the Sadducees in: 1) their expectation of a coming messiah who would set the Israelites free from Roman rule and bring all Israelites back together, and 2) their belief in life after death, a belief that many scholars think may have come with the Israelites when they returned to Judea from captivity in Babylonia (598–538 BC).

There was one other group that that held sway among first-century Israelites, called **Zealots.** They were vehemently opposed to Roman rule, and some of them were willing and ready to engage in violence and acts of terrorism against Rome and against Israelites who were too yielding to the Romans. They were the leaders of the revolt against Rome in AD 66–70 that led the Romans to destroy the Temple. In AD 73, in the aftermath of the revolt against Rome at Masada, the Zealots committed

---

11. Kaufmann Kohler, "Sadducees," *Jewish Encyclopedia,* https://www.jewish-encyclopedia.com/articles/12989-Sadducees.

suicide rather than surrender to Roman rule. Shaye I.D. Cohen, the Samuel Ungerleider Professor of Judaic Studies and Professor of Religious Studies Brown University, says the following about the Zealots:

> [The Zealots] took their religious understanding of what Judaism was, took their religious interpretations and turned that into a political agenda. "We must destroy the Roman Empire or we must destroy Jews who cooperate with the Roman Empire. We will kill all collaborators, no King but God," and other such slogans emerge from these religious thinkers.[12]

It is important to hold the Zealots in mind as we examine the life of Jesus, because their worldview, as well as others, shaped the dynamic of the circumstances of Jesus' life and ministry.

In the Gospels, the Pharisees are often presented in a most negative fashion. The Essenes and Zealots are not mentioned, but their influence is implicit. Most Christians have assumed a very negative view of the Pharisees. I have often harped on the point that, in the Gospels, the only people toward whom Jesus expresses significant anger are the Pharisees. However, I take a different route in this book, in light of a four-part twist, most of which comes from Rabbi Joseph Telushkin.

The first part of the twist is the fact that the Pharisees are the only group that survived past the first part of the second century. What we know as Judaism comes from the Pharisees. The Pharisaic viewpoint and perspective became Judaism as we know it.

Second, what we know about the other groups, especially the Sadducees, comes from the Pharisees. We read about the Sadducees through the lens of their rivals.

Third, our image of the Pharisees today is influenced by our idiomatic usage of the word as it developed throughout history:

> Unfortunately, at the very time all Jews were increasingly identifying as Pharisees, the word began to acquire a new, highly pejorative meaning. The New Testament repeatedly depicted the Pharisees as small-minded religious hypocrites. Eventually, the word "pharisee" came to be synonymous in English with "hypocrite"—a distortion as obnoxious to Jews as the expression "to jew," meaning "to bargain down or to cheat."[13]

---

12. Shaye I.D. Cohen, "Frontline: From Jesus to Christ," WGBH Educational Foundation (published April 1998) https://www.pbs.org/wgbh/pages/frontline/shows/religion/portrait/judaism.html.

13. Telushkin, *Jewish Literacy*, 127.

5

The fourth part of the twist is an observation from some of my friends who are Jewish rabbis. Although there is an explicit polemic presented in the Gospels between Jesus and his fellow Israelites, it is also true that this was an intra-faith fight. Jesus was not starting a new religion. He was born an Israelite and died an Israelite. So, while Jesus was different among his fellow Israelites, he was still interpreting and living Israelite faith. So I ask my rabbi friends, "Among these four groups—the Sadducees, the Pharisees, the Essenes, and the Zealots—with which group was Jesus most closely aligned?" Every one of them has said that Jesus most closely aligns with the Pharisees. This insight forever changes how I will read the Gospels and understand Jesus.

The Pharisees, like Jesus, assigned authority to the interpretation of the Torah and Mosaic Law. For example, in multiple places in the Gospels, we read where Jesus says, "You have heard it said . . . but I say unto you . . ." (e.g., Matthew 5:38-48). We also read about times when people said Jesus taught "with authority," probably meaning, he taught with authority equal to that of the Torah and Law. At least, it means that he taught with authority equal to the authority of the most respected scribes of the time (see Matthew 7:29; Mark 1:22). This is essentially a Pharisaic perspective regarding oral teachings on Mosaic Law.

In some sense, Jesus' fiercest battle was with the group with which he was most closely aligned. This means that the polemic between Jesus and the Pharisees is not a rejection of them. It's a disagreement that grows out of a fundamental agreement about interpreting, guiding, teaching, and living Israelite faith.

Roman Rule and Hellenistic Culture

First-century Israelite faith was practiced under Roman rule and within a web of Hellenistic culture. Roman rule meant oppressive taxes and a pressure to practice allegiance to and worship of the Roman emperor. Hellenistic culture meant that Israelite life and beliefs were constantly mixed with and influenced by Greek ideals. This is the world, primarily, into which Jesus was born, and in which he lived and died as an Israelite. We must never neglect this truth as we explore who Jesus was, who he is, and how we can recognize him as our own Lord and Savior.

Next, we turn to examining more closely how Jesus understood, interpreted, reinterpreted, and lived his faith.

6

DIVINE

For in him all the fullness of God was pleased to dwell.
—Colossians 1:19, NRSV

The impact of Jesus gets impeded by our rejection or distortion of his divinity. How do the Gospels present Jesus as Divine?

According to John's Gospel account, Jesus told the disciples that there are more things to learn about him not revealed during Jesus' earthly life. These things would be revealed later by the Holy Spirit (John 16:12-15). I believe that the Church's creeds and historical doctrines are examples of this ongoing work of the Holy Spirit to reveal the truth and mysteries of Jesus.

However, I also believe that we must engage with the first and earliest witness to Jesus, particularly the witness given in the Gospels. In this chapter, I want to present Jesus from the witness of the Gospels while acknowledging how the Church's creeds and doctrines have helped us interpret and understand the Gospels.

When we read the Gospels, it becomes apparent that, while they present a unified story about Jesus, their stories occasionally vary in the details. These differences work to show us different sides and dimensions of Jesus, which turns out to be a great benefit to us. Rather than seeing the differences in the Gospel stories as tensions to be resolved, we should embrace them as beautiful gifts to us. Through their differences, we get a fuller, more expansive, and richer picture of Jesus.

The Gospel Witness to Jesus' Divinity

The Gospels differ in how they tell Jesus' story and how they understand and describe his divinity. Yet they do agree on this idea about Jesus: in and through him, people experienced a presence, a glory, a power, and a love that they had previously experienced as the presence of God. The Gospels communicate this in many ways. Matthew and Luke give us stories about Jesus being conceived by the Holy Spirit rather than through human conception. In Matthew's account, people worship Jesus in the same way they would worship God (see Matthew 2:11; 28:8-9; Luke 24:52). Matthew, Mark, and Luke all give stories of God making special appearances at Jesus' baptism to affirm him having a unique relationship with God.

John describes the divine aspect of Jesus in a different, more philosophical way. But no matter which Gospel you read, all four Gospels clearly instruct us that, in Jesus of Nazareth, God was present in a new and decisive way.

I turn, now, to the Gospel of John because John gives us the boldest witness to Jesus' divinity, and more important, he gives us, I suggest, the most effective word-image for understanding how Jesus revealed the heart and nature of God.

> In the beginning was the Word, and the Word was with God, and the Word was God. He was in the beginning with God. All things were made through Him, and without Him nothing was made that was made. In Him was life, and the life was the light of men. And the light shines in the darkness, and the darkness did not comprehend it.
>
> There was a man sent from God, whose name was John. This man came for a witness, to bear witness of the Light, that all through him might believe. He was not that Light, but was sent to bear witness of that Light. That was the true Light which gives light to every man coming into the world.
>
> He was in the world, and the world was made through Him, and the world did not know Him. He came to His own, and His own did not receive Him. But as many as received Him, to them He gave the right to become children of God, to those who believe in His name: who were born, not of blood, nor of the will of the flesh, nor of the will of man, but of God.

> And the Word became flesh and dwelt among us, and we beheld
> His glory, the glory as of the only begotten of the Father, full of grace and
> truth. (John 1:1-14)

First, I want to acknowledge that, for the Israelites, it was blasphemous to say that God became a human being or that a human being is God. Any interpretation of how the Pharisees and Sadducees responded to Jesus needs to take this fact into consideration. Those who rejected Jesus were not consciously rejecting God. They were striving to be loyal to a core principle of Israelite faith. For the Israelites of Jesus' time, God is not any human being, and no human being is God.

The claim that John makes here is that the Word entered human history through the person of Jesus of Nazareth. Historians of the ancient world tell us that this claim—the Word, personified—would not have been strange to the Israelites of Palestine (or to the Romans and Hellenists). The actual Greek word used by John, here, is *Logos*, which is multilayered in meaning. It can be "word," "speech," "account," "story," or "message."[1] It can also mean thought, meaning, reason, principle, logic, and divine wisdom, divine word, or divine truth.[2] I list these varied interpretations of *logos* to invite you to think and reflect on all of them in relation to John's use of the term. I suggest that all of them can be helpful in getting to the depth of what it means to say that Jesus is the Word of God. So, rather than seeing these as competing interpretations, see them as complementary insights.

The way that John talks about the *Logos* is similar to Wisdom's self-description in Proverbs 8:22-31:

"The LORD possessed me at the beginning of His way,

Before His works of old.

I have been established from everlasting,

From the beginning, before there was ever an earth.

When there were no depths I was brought forth,

When there were no fountains abounding with water.

Before the mountains were settled,

---

1.   David H. Johnson, "Logos," *Dictionary of Jesus & the Gospels* (Downers Grove, IL: Intervarsity Press, 1992), 481.

2.   *New World Encyclopedia*, s.v. "Logos," accessed November 2, 2021, https://www.newworldencyclopedia.org/p/index.php?title=Logos&oldid=1013090.

Before the hills, I was brought forth;

While as yet He had not made the earth or the fields,

Or the primal dust of the world.

When He prepared the heavens, I was there,

When He drew a circle on the face of the deep,

When He established the clouds above,

When He strengthened the fountains of the deep,

When He assigned to the sea its limit,

So that the waters would not transgress His command,

When He marked out the foundations of the earth,

Then I was beside Him as a master craftsman;

And I was daily His delight,

Rejoicing always before Him,

Rejoicing in His inhabited world,

And my delight was with the sons of men."

In this self-description, Wisdom is personified, but in John 1, we see something else, something more: the Word of God is said to have become flesh in a particular person, in a particular time, and in a particular place. John's use of the word *logos* is particularly helpful because it encompasses all the ways the Gospels envision Jesus as divine. God was present in Jesus because the Word—God's expression, God's wisdom, God's mediating vehicle, God's generative and regenerative power, and God's saving agency—*tabernacled* in Jesus. "For in him all the fullness of God was pleased to dwell." (Colossians 1:19, NRSV).

The Word Became Flesh. So What?

What can we learn about God through the revelation of Jesus as God's Word? If Jesus was the expression, wisdom, mediating vehicle, and saving agency of God "with us," then he gives us a living demonstration of the heart and mind of God. This is how Jesus expressed it to one of his disciples:

Philip said, "Lord, show us the Father and that will be enough for us."

Jesus answered: "Don't you know me, Philip, even after I have been among you such a long time? Anyone who has seen me has seen the Father. How can you say, 'Show us the Father'? Don't you believe that I am in the Father, and that the Father is in me? The words I say to you I do not speak on my own authority. Rather, it is the Father, living in me, who is doing his work. Believe me when I say that I am in the Father and the Father is in me (John 14:8-11a, NIV).

Jesus is telling Phillip, and us, that what was seen and experienced of him during his time on earth reflects the heart and mind of God.

It is particularly interesting that the Church, especially in our times, so often engages in worshiping Jesus with barely any acknowledgment of the kind of God Jesus reveals. It's like saying that you are in love with a person, but you don't really know anything about the person, and you have no interest in learning anything about the person. Without knowing anything about the person you claim to love, you are most likely infatuated with your own ideas, fantasies, and imaginations about the person. A great many segments of the Church worship Jesus as God but ignore the things that Jesus revealed to us about God. Instead of worshiping the God who came through Jesus, they worship their ideas, fantasies, and imaginations about God.

Throughout the millennia, we have wrapped Jesus in our ideas, fantasies, imaginations, dogmas, and doctrines; we have lifted him *high*, disconnected from anything related to his actual life and, often, our own lives. The further we push Jesus into a spiritual, esoteric, ethereal, and celestial existence, the more we love him in comfort. People love a god who receives adulation without "sticking God's hands" into our lives except to rescue us from danger. People love a god whom they can build from their imaginations instead of God who holds them accountable to a standard for humanity. (Read Exodus 32 for a biblical example of how people prefer to build their own gods rather than submit to the God whom they cannot control and who makes demands on their humanity). All over the world today, people gather in the name of Jesus to engage in practices and cultivate worldviews that are all contrary to the God who was revealed in Jesus.

With as little reference as we make to what actually happened when "the Word became flesh dwelt among us," to the actual life that Jesus lived as a revelation of God's mind and heart, we might as well be worshiping any random deity, any celestial being, or any arbitrary, transcendent power. If we, in our worship and our lives, aren't shaped by the actual revelation of God that came through Jesus, then we aren't really worshiping Jesus or the God whom Jesus revealed. Rather, we are merely using Jesus' name as a label and cover for the true gods of our hearts: power, status, wealth, success, fame, safety, individualism, race, nationality, anger, revenge, war, ourselves, and so on. We have taken the name that Paul says is "the name which is above every name" (Philippians 2:9) and projected it onto our idols, gods that are diametrically opposed to Jesus' life, teachings, and mission. We have taken the name of Jesus in vain.

Also, when Christians disconnect the Jesus of our worship from Jesus, the Word made flesh, I believe that we handicap our witness about Jesus. I am confident that, if more of the world knew about Jesus' earthly life, ministry, and teachings and not just the Jesus of our creeds, doctrines, and dogmas, they would be drawn to him and would open their hearts to him. The Word made flesh, as presented in the Gospels, speaks to the human condition as nothing else can or does.

So, to avoid this error of disconnecting Christian worship from the God revealed through Jesus, we must try to give some answers to this question: "What did we learn about God when God's Word became flesh and dwelt with us?"

God Who Is with Us and beyond Us

When the Word became flesh and dwelt among us as Jesus, it affirmed the Israelites' experience of God who is with us and who shows up in particular, ordinary, and unlikely locations. The Israelites of Jesus' time would view as blasphemous the claim that Jesus was "God with us" (*Immanuel*; Matthew 1:23). But according to the Israelite story of faith, the presence of God had shown up and abided (tabernacled) in places no more holy than a human life. I even suggest that it is God's Presence that makes a place or a person holy. The ordinary places where God shows up are often the most unlikely of places, but God's presence lends to them an extraordinary holiness and sacredness.

I am not equating all the locations of God with God's location in Jesus. As a Christian, I believe that Jesus is God's ultimate and decisive location. However, God's location in Jesus of Nazareth was, indeed, a continuation of a worldview in which God manifests in ordinary and unlikely places, and in unusual ways, so that we might experience Divine presence and glimpse Divine glory. I am not referring merely to God's communication with human beings, but to stories in which God tabernacles (dwells) in or regularly visits a particular location. In these situations, God's people could say, "We can find God here."

Moses encounters Divine presence in a burning bush (Exodus 3:1-6). When the Israelites were fleeing from slavery in Egypt and being pursued by the Egyptian soldiers, God showed up in a pillar of cloud and a pillar of fire (Exodus 13:21-22). God showed up on Mount Sinai and even made it, for a while, God's dwelling place (Exodus 3:12; 19–40). While on Mount Sinai, God showed up as a cloud in an ordinary tent (Exodus 33:7-11).

Additionally, while on Mount Sinai, God had Moses and the Israelites to construct a "special box"—the ark of the covenant—where God's presence would dwell. When the time came to leave the holy mountain, they were to take God's presence, in the box, with them.

Sometime around the late first century BC, God could be found in the body of a baby lying in a manger. A little later, this baby was in the arms of his mother as she and her husband were refugees, fleeing to Egypt to escape genocide. Even later, this baby would become a young adult undergoing a horrible crucifixion.

In all these ways and places, God showed up. God shows up in our world, today, in the most unlikely of locations, and like the people in the Bible, we are constantly surprised by where God manifests. For example, I am encountering God, these days, through the music of Kanye West. The secular, unchurched story, told through his most recent music, of being transformed by the relentless love of God is astonishing.

In the Israelite story, a prophet named Isaiah had an encounter with God in the Temple and is given the secret to top all secrets. It is a secret that will shatter shallow religion: **The whole earth is full of God's glory** (Isaiah 6:1-3)! There's no telling where God might show up! With all due respect to the things and places we view as channels for encountering God—Eastern Orthodoxy, the Catholic Church, the multiple Protestant denominations, the undeniable beauty of million-dollar sanctuaries, the pope, bishops, evangelists, prophets, pastors, superin-tendents, faith-healers, church altars, prayer rooms, and pulpits—what those angels told Isaiah, some 2,500 years ago, may not change the need for prayer rooms and pulpits; but if we don't grasp what these angels told that prophet, we probably can't maximize the full power of our prayer rooms and pulpits.

Right now, in this very moment, pause and ponder places where you encounter the Divine presence. Some will feel ordinary, but don't discount the unlikely sources of Divine encounters. They are just as real, and they are consistent with the story of Jesus and the how he mediated the presence of God as the Word made flesh. God is with us.

Yet God is also beyond us. Theologians refer to this as God's *transcendence*. Regardless of where or how God shows up to be with us, no location or manifestation of God can give us a full grasp, control, or apprehension of God. One way the Bible shows this is in how God moves around as God determines. God changes locations (dwelling place) multiple times to meet the needs of Divine mission. Notice this in my list above of places where God shows up. God is moving around, and Christians now believe that God dwells in us as we live in the world as the body of Christ. In Revelation, we are told that we will dwell in a new holy city, the new Jerusalem (Revelation 21). God graces us with Divine Presence but is never locked into or chained by a place, a person, a form, or a way of appearance.

By the way, we experience the same thing with one another. No matter how close we are to another person, if we pay attention, there is always a side, a dimension, a kind of *otherness* to the person that we cannot reach or fathom. I have heard youth use a phrase to draw bound-aries with their family members and friends who try to get into their *otherness*. They will say, "Hey! Don't come at me like you know me!" I love this strong, symbolic language. We know each other, and yet we are forever strangers. It's the mystery of divinity as well as humanness.

As God shows up in the world to be with us; God also moves out and away from locations that we have treasured as trustworthy media-tors of God's presence. It is very tempting and easy to turn a vessel of God's manifestation into an idol.

For example, in nearly every church where I have served, there were traditions, people, experiences through which God had manifested, and those manifestations become sacred vessels for those believers, sources of the Divine that they held onto as if for dear life. Sometimes, however, God had moved on from those vessels. They were no longer glowing with God's light or brimming with God's power. In nearly every such case, the members in those local churches struggled greatly to let go of those vessels and move, with God, on to new vessels and new locations of God's presence. In many cases, they held onto the vessels God had deserted to the point of death.

We can't chain God in any one place, moment, or source of God's *nearness*. God moves. I have mentioned the story of God's presence at Mount Sinai, which was, as we might imagine, an amazing blessing for the Israelites. Mount Sinai was a sacred place. How could it not be when you got to experience the nearness of God with your community, in a particular place, with clear expectations, daily provisions, and a dynamic leader in Moses? Nevertheless, God determined to move, and, according to Deuteronomy 6:6-8, God had to command them to leave the mountain with Him.

> "At Mount Horeb the LORD our God spoke to us. He said, 'You have stayed at this mountain long enough. Go to the hill country where the Amorites live and to all the neighboring areas in the Jordan Valley, the hill country, the western slopes, the Negev, and the seacoast. Go throughout the land of Canaan and Lebanon as far as the great river, the Euphrates. Look, I am giving you this land. Go and take it. It is the land that I, the LORD, promised to give to your ancestors—Abraham, Isaac, and Jacob. I promised to give this land to them and to their descendants.'" (ERV)

God blesses us in a place or situation. We get attached to it. God determines to move from that place or situation, but we cling to it anyway. We chain ourselves to a situational blessing. So God has to push us away from that place or situation so that we can experience and enjoy a greater purpose and a greater blessing. If only we could embrace the truth that God moves, we would move with God and get to our greater purposes, quicker and with far less damage. Nothing can separate us from God's loving presence, but we can't chain God's love and presence to one specific situation. Everything changes, and God is faithful in all circumstances.

We have to regularly examine our lives, our relationships, and our varied communities and ask these tough questions: 1) Is God still at work through this vessel? 2) What are the new and different ways that God has chosen to use as mediators of Divine presence?

The inability to lock God into any one manifestation includes God-inspired language and concepts. Whatever we say and think about God is limited. If we try to turn our language and ideas into an exact statement about God, they become impediments to people being able to experience God in ways that are not captured by our language and concepts. We know that we are in spiritual danger whenever we begin to think that, by our knowledge and experiences of Jesus, we have fully grasped him.

In Jesus, God's mobility, God's nearness, and God's mystery are all highlighted and maximized. God was as near to us as ever; yet 2,000 years later, we are still trying to get a grasp of Jesus. In Jesus, God is both our friend and the eternal Word at the same time; in Jesus we find the one appearance of God that is steady and true for all time.

A God of Disruptive Love

If Jesus of Nazareth was a living demonstration of the heart and mind of God, then we learn from Jesus that God is surprising and disruptive for the world, and that includes the Church as we know it today.

The defining characteristic of the God revealed in Jesus is *love*. Love defines Jesus. Not judgment, power, holiness, justice, righteousness, anger, or law and order, but love. For sure, these other dimensions of God are present in the person of Jesus, but they are channeled and filtered through God's love. John 3:16 articulates this explicitly, saying that God's intervening presence in the world, through Jesus, is because, "God so loved the world" (NRSV).

Any person who wants to try to bear witness from a Christian perspective to what they think God is doing in the world has to begin and end with God's Love. To do otherwise is to bear an anti-Christian witness. Unfortunately, such witness happens a lot, and the spiritual, emotional, and relational consequences are devastating and long-lasting. All across the world, the influence and impact of God remains unrecognized, because God is presented as something, or someone, other than the God of love. I think about people I've known who grew up hearing a lot of preaching about the anger and judgment of God, so they grew up feeling guilty, ashamed, and judged. No matter how many times they went to the altar of a church to confess and repent, they couldn't shake those feelings of guilt, shame, judgment, and impending death. If you

6

live with that kind of despair long enough, it can provoke you to suicide, either physical or spiritual.

It was perfectly fitting for Jesus to label his message to the world as "good news." It was good news—it is good news—because the core message of Jesus' saving sacrifice and resurrection life is that God loves us, all of us, all of creation. If Jesus' followers are going to be faithful to Jesus and the God Jesus shows us, we have to be relentless to ensure that this fundamental, core message constructs, instructs, and manages our witness (sermons, music, teaching, community service, mentoring, coaching, counseling). It is very easy for us to fall into the trap of allowing our witness, our acts of ministry, to flow from places within us and among us that are fearful, insecure, angry, bitter, vengeful, competitive, lustful, or depressed. Our witness must not be shaped by these feelings and inclinations. Instead, we need to allow God's love to shape the content, tone, and the *touch* of our witness.

According to the Gospels, Jesus was sent by God as an expression of God's love. Jesus isn't just a witness to God's love; Jesus is God's love in the flesh. Jesus is a demonstration of God's love. Jesus is God's best love letter to the world. We are to interpret everything that Jesus does as God's attempt to love us and communicate God's love for us. We should read the Gospels as narratives about God's love.

According to God's love as Jesus, God's love is self-sacrificing for the sake of others to the point of giving up divine status and privilege. Paul expounds on this idea powerfully in Philippians 2:5-11. Paul's essential message in this passage is that, in an act of self-sacrificing love, Jesus gives up Divine status to become a human servant, obeying the Father's will to the point of death on a cross.

According to God's love as Jesus, God's love is risk-taking for the sake of others, to the point of God placing God's self in the hands of human beings. This is part of the essential beauty of the Christmas and Resurrection stories. God's love takes the risk of being born as an infant who is vulnerable to both the care of human hands and the threat of human hate.[3] Then God's love surrenders to human authorities and becomes vulnerable to crucifixion and a grave. This is what God's love looks like at work on behalf of God's creation. The love of God risks and is vulnerable!

---

3. See Matthew 2 for Herod's hate.

64

According to God's love in the person of Jesus, God's love is authentic and transparent to the point of publicly communicating some of God's plans and expressing deep emotions (e.g., Matthew 9:35-38; Mark 1:14-15; Luke 4:16-20; 10:21; 19:41-44; John 2:13-17; 11:35).

According to God's love as Jesus, God is calling, guiding, and empowering all of creation to fulfill God's purposes. Matthew tells us that Jesus himself was sent by God to save people from sin, or "missing the mark" of who we were created to be (Matthew 1:21).[4]

According to God's love as Jesus, God's love is extended to all of creation, not just human beings. God loves the world (John 3:16). Through his parables and actions, Jesus lives out God's love as a presence that encourages and empowers purpose for nature and peaceful unity between nature and human beings (e.g., Matthew 13:24-30; Mark 4; 11:12-25; Luke 13:6-9).

According to God's love expressed through Jesus, God's love is relentless and unyielding, especially in pursuit of the most broken of people. God leaves the community of ninety-nine sheep to go find the one sheep that has gotten lost. God searches in the darkness for lost coins. God gives human beings freedom to make choices, and, if they make the wrong choices, God waits patiently for them to return home. When they return, instead of treating them as wayward children, God "throws a party" to celebrate their return (Luke 15).

According to God's love as Jesus, when people fail, miserably, God's love shows up on the *seashores* of their lives and give them permission to go back and try again (John 21:1-10).

According to God's love as Jesus, God's love hosts great parties and banquets and invites all the outcasts and untouchables of society to dine with him (Matthew 22:1-14; Luke 14:15-24).

According to God's love as Jesus, the goal of God's love isn't to keep us safe. Rather, God's love makes us dangerous to evil powers and systems (Matthew 10:5-8; 16:17-19; Mark 16:14-18; Luke 10:1-24).

According to God's love as Jesus, the love of God pushes us into storms to strengthen our faith, our confidence, and our humanity (Mat-

---

4. "Missing the mark" is my theological understanding of the essential nature of sin. To hear a fuller exploration of "missing the mark" as the essence of sin, see Jonathan Silver, "Podcast: David Bashevkin on Sin and Failure in Jewish Thought," October 3, 2019, in *The Tikvah Podcast*, podcast, MP3 audio, 35:38, https://tikvah.libsyn.com/david-bashevkin-on-sin-and-failure-in-jewish-thought.

6

thew 14:22-33). Jesus didn't pamper and pet his disciples. Rather, he equipped and encouraged them to face challenges with faith, courage, confidence, and creativity. This is how he loved them.

Through Jesus, we see what God's love is up against. Jesus got angry when he saw religious hypocrisy and the use of religion to oppress people (Matthew 23; John 8:1-11). In one of his "mission statements," Jesus announced that he was empowered by God's Spirit to come against poverty, brokenheartedness, human bondage, blindness, oppression, and oppressive debt (Luke 4:16-19). Jesus got angry when he saw religious leaders engaging in unjust financial practices and religious manipulation in the Temple (Matthew 21:12–17, Mark 11:15–19, Luke 19:45–48; John 2:13–16). Jesus was against unproductivity, especially when it came from a place of privilege (Matthew 25:14-30; Mark 1:12-25; Luke 13:6-9). Jesus was against sickness and disease (apparent throughout the Gospels), and, of course, Jesus was fundamentally opposed to satan and the powers and forces of evil. In fact, just his arrival at a place would arouse fierce reactions from the demonic presences, which shows, by the way, how unwelcoming the world had/has become toward God's love (Mark 3:11-12; John 3:16-21).

As God's love in the flesh, Jesus was heartbroken over missed opportunities and wasted potential (Matthew 23:37-39; Luke 19:41-44).

And God's love is for everyone.

The God Who Is for All People

According to God's love as Jesus, God's love is inclusive of all people. The expression of God that came through Jesus was an affirmation of what the Israelites had already known, that through the Israelites God would bless all people. Much of what Jesus said and did was the fulfilling of that promise. Jesus was almost constantly bringing the blessing of Abraham to everyone he encountered, regardless of their national or social identity. Standing firmly in his Israelite identity and confidently claiming to speak on behalf of the God of Israel, Jesus said:

> Come to Me, all you who labor and are heavy laden, and I will give you rest. Take My yoke upon you and learn from Me, for I am gentle and lowly in heart, and you will find rest for your souls (Matthew 11:28-29).

6

thew 14:22-33). Jesus didn't pamper and pet his disciples. Rather, he equipped and encouraged them to face challenges with faith, courage, confidence, and creativity. This is how he loved them.

Through Jesus, we see what God's love is up against. Jesus got angry when he saw religious hypocrisy and the use of religion to oppress people (Matthew 23; John 8:1-11). In one of his "mission statements," Jesus announced that he was empowered by God's Spirit to come against poverty, brokenheartedness, human bondage, blindness, oppression, and oppressive debt (Luke 4:16-19). Jesus got angry when he saw religious leaders engaging in unjust financial practices and religious manipulation in the Temple (Matthew 21:12–17, Mark 11:15–19, Luke 19:45–48; John 2:13–16). Jesus was against unproductivity, especially when it came from a place of privilege (Matthew 25:14-30; Mark 1:12-25; Luke 13:6-9). Jesus was against sickness and disease (apparent throughout the Gospels), and, of course, Jesus was fundamentally opposed to satan and the powers and forces of evil. In fact, just his arrival at a place would arouse fierce reactions from the demonic presences, which shows, by the way, how unwelcoming the world had/has become toward God's love (Mark 3:11-12; John 3:16-21).

As God's love in the flesh, Jesus was heartbroken over missed opportunities and wasted potential (Matthew 23:37-39; Luke 19:41-44).

And God's love is for everyone.

The God Who Is for All People

According to God's love as Jesus, God's love is inclusive of all people. The expression of God that came through Jesus was an affirmation of what the Israelites had already known, that through the Israelites God would bless all people. Much of what Jesus said and did was the fulfilling of that promise. Jesus was almost constantly bringing the blessing of Abraham to everyone he encountered, regardless of their national or social identity. Standing firmly in his Israelite identity and confidently claiming to speak on behalf of the God of Israel, Jesus said:

> Come to Me, all you who labor and are heavy laden, and I will give you rest. Take My yoke upon you and learn from Me, for I am gentle and lowly in heart, and you will find rest for your souls (Matthew 11:28-29).

222222

Jesus never tries to abolish or diminish the laws and practices of his faith community. Rather, he wraps them in the Abrahamic promise to bless all people. The God who exclusively chose the Israelites is radically inclusive, and this is demonstrated through Jesus. For Jesus, this is the point of the Israelites being God's chosen people. This is the goal toward which all of Israelite history was reaching, that, through God's chosen people Israel, God would redeem all of creation.

In his conversation with Nicodemus, Jesus describes God as the God who deeply loves the whole world, which we should take to mean, all people and all of creation (John 3:16). This isn't radical for an Israelite. This is fulfillment of the covenant with Abraham.

I acknowledge that there is a definite dimension to Israelite faith that asserts a belief that God blesses those who obey God's laws and rejects those who disobey, and that the blessings of God are for God's chosen people. Psalm 1 is a great example of this:

Blessed is the one
> who does not walk in step with the wicked
or stand in the way that sinners take
> or sit in the company of mockers,
but whose delight is in the law of the LORD,
> and who meditates on his law day and night.
That person is like a tree planted by streams of water,
> which yields its fruit in season
and whose leaf does not wither—
> whatever they do prospers.
Not so the wicked!
> They are like chaff
that the wind blows away.
Therefore the wicked will not stand in the judgment,
> nor sinners in the assembly of the righteous.
For the LORD watches over the way of the righteous,
> but the way of the wicked leads to destruction. (NIV)

However, the real-life experiences of the Israelites taught them that God cannot be chained to a *black-and-white* dynamic. Their experience of Egyptian slavery, their constant battles with foreign nations, the destruction of the Northern Kingdom and then the Southern Kingdom, the taking of God's people into captivity, and, especially, the experiences of seeing the Temple invaded, exploited, and, even destroyed reminded them that God loves all people, not just them. In contrast to, but included in the Israelites' songbook, along with Psalm 1 is Psalm 73, which speaks of how, sometimes, "the wicked" enjoy prosperity:

> Surely God is good to Israel,
>> to those who are pure in heart.
> But as for me, my feet had almost slipped;
>> I had nearly lost my foothold.
> For I envied the arrogant
>> when I saw the prosperity of the wicked.
> They have no struggles;
>> their bodies are healthy and strong.
> They are free from common human burdens;
>> they are not plagued by human ills. (Psalm 73:1-5, NIV)

This psalm reflects what the Israelites are figuring out, though not fully yet, that God loves and blesses all people, including their enemies. When Jesus comes, he reveals this truth in its fullness. When he calls for a new standard of love, that is, to love even one's enemies, the motivation he uses is that loving your enemies makes you "children of your Father in heaven" (Matthew 5:45a, NRSV). This isn't a new thing about God or from God. It is the fulfillment of the promise in the Abrahamic covenant to "bless all the people of the earth."

Glory, Grace, and Truth

What did we learn about God when God's Word became flesh and dwelt with us? We learn from Jesus how to better detect when we are experiencing God's glory. John tells us that, when God's glory was revealed through Jesus, it ushered in grace and truth (John 1:14).

The glory of God is so important to the entire biblical story that you could use it as a lens for understanding and interpreting Bible.[5]

5.   "With references in English Bibles ranging from 275 (NIV) to 350 (RSV),

On one hand, throughout the Bible, people encountered the presence and glory of God and often remained oblivious to it or unmoved by it. Jacob testified that he had been in the very presence of God and did not know it (Genesis 28:16). The Israelites were privy to God's glory at Mount Sinai, yet they built an idol—a golden calf—in the very shadow of that glory.

On the other hand, on the back side of the Midian desert, Moses had the wherewithal to pay attention to God's presence in a burning bush. When Elisha is surrounded by the Syrians in a military battle, he prays that his fretful and fearful servant would be able to see what he already could see, that they are being protected by a supernatural army (see 2 Kings 6). God was there. One person could see God's glory, but the other person was oblivious to it.

Isn't it interesting how two people can look at the same thing but see something totally different?

You see the same kind of conflicting perceptions when God's glory shows up in "Jesus." Some people, in fact, some deeply religious people, encounter Jesus and see a glutton and a winebibber (Matthew 11:19). Other people see him casting out a demon and they say Jesus is possessed by a demon (Mark 3:20-27). When a Roman soldier watches Jesus dying on a cross, he sees a totally different reality: "Truly, this man was the Son of God!" (Mark 15:39). It's the same Jesus, and it's the same glory, but not everyone *sees* it or is moved by it. How can we get better at not missing God's glory among us? The writer of the Gospel of John gives us a clue about how to know when we are in a moment of Divine glory. When God tabernacled among us through Jesus of Nazareth, the glory of God was made visible with two signs: grace and truth.

glory is one of the master images that helps to tell the story of the Bible. A survey of the references yields a tour of some of the Bible's great moments—from the giving of the law (Ex 24:12-18), to the wilderness wanderings of Israel (Num 14:10, 21, 22; 16:19, 42; 20:6), to the worship of God in the tabernacle (Lev 9:6, 23) and temple (1 Kings 8:11; 2 Chron 5:14), to the call and prophetic vision of the prophets Isaiah (Is 6) and Ezekiel (Ezek 1), to the birth (Lk 2:9) and transfiguration of Jesus (Lk 9:31; 2 Pet 1:7), to the final, apocalyptic scene of the holy city Jerusalem descending in the clouds (Rev 21:23-34)" ("Glory," *Dictionary of Biblical Imagery* [Downers Grove, IL: InterVarsity Press, 2010], 330, Kindle).

Grace and Truth

Grace is God's loving-kindness toward us. Sometimes, it shows up as mercy. Sometimes, it's pure, unmerited favor, giving us goodness and good things that we don't deserve and haven't earned. Grace is God giving us the capacity to do what we cannot do on our own.

The great religious leader, John Wesley, found it impossible to talk and think about life and faith outside of the parameters of grace. This is why Methodists, Wesley's spiritual descendants, have crafted a religious framework that's anchored in the power of grace:

- Prevenient Grace—God's love and kindness toward us before we ever acknowledge or turn to God.

- Justifying Grace—the Love by which we are adopted into God's family at the very moment that we turn to and surrender to God, no matter how feeble is the turn or how unstable is the surrender.

- Sanctifying Grace—the Love of God that turns our moment of surrender into a journey of cooperation with the Holy Spirit's faithful work of transformation and maturation in our lives.

There's no dimension of life not covered by God's grace. It's the *ocean* into which we were born and live out our lives.

When I think about grace, I think about Remy, the rat in the Disney movie, *Ratatouille.* When the movie begins, Remy and his family are living beneath the streets of a city, in the sewer, as rats do, but on an adventure to find food, Remy gets separated from his family, gets lost, and ends up journeying up to street level. He climbs to the rooftop of a building, looks out, and sees the Eiffel Tower, which he had known about only from watching his favorite chef on television. When he sees the Eiffel Tower, he realizes where he is: in Paris! Remy realizes that he has spent all his life living in the sewers of Paris, in the shadow of the Eiffel Tower. This is how life is for us as God children. We dwell in the *sewers* of existence, not realizing that, the entire time, we are surrounded by God's grace. Wherever Glory shows up, Grace is always there.

Truth is harder to define because most of us have been taught that, or nurtured to live as if, truth is relative, that there is no such thing as objective truth, or that truth is a matter of a set of facts. Let me be clear so as not to be confused with those folks who relentlessly deny facts. Facts matter! However, you can have all the *facts* about something and still not know *truth*. At least, you may not have truth in the deepest sense. There's truth, and then, there's TRUTH. From a biblical perspective, from the perspective of the writer of the Gospel of John, truth is about the essence of a thing. Truth includes fact, but it's always more. Truth is facts, plus what they mean. Truth is facts, plus the reality to which the facts, as signs, point. Truth is there, abiding, with or without facts.

A husband or wife can ask a spouse, "Are you having an affair?" The spouse can give facts that support the answer, but that doesn't get the couple to truth. The truth is that the couple is in a state of estrangement, alienation, broken intimacy, and lack of trust. The spouse asking the question is looking for facts—data—to help get a grasp of their shared truth.

A student can make a *C* in a college course, and that would be a fact. However, the *C* doesn't necessarily tell the truth about how much the student has learned or been transformed by the course.

Facts are truth trying to reveal itself to beings who are trapped and chained by linear thinking. This is why emotions can often get us to truth in a way that facts cannot. This is, no doubt, a dangerous statement to make in these times, when people, drowning in emotional chaos, deny facts or twist facts to fit their twisted agendas. So let's be clear. Emotions can sometimes get us to truth better than logic can, but the truth—if it's the truth—will make sense of the facts.

Truth is the reality of who we are. Truth is the reality of our relationships and our circumstance. This is how Jesus is the Truth. Jesus isn't a conglomeration of facts about life; he's the Truth about life. Jesus isn't a set of facts of human nature; he's the Truth about what it means to be fully human. Jesus isn't data about God; he's the Truth about who God is. Jesus may not speak to the details of your circumstances, but he will tell you the Truth about your circumstances.

Truth, real Truth, most often, transcends language, speech, and logic. To be given, truth has to be imparted, infused, *seeded*, and "breathed" (see John 20:21-23). To receive it, we have to *inhale* it, meditate on it, be impregnated with it, or be permeated by it.

Symbols, metaphors, and stories can open doorways to truth in ways that facts, logic, and linear thinking cannot. And wherever Glory shows up, Truth is present.

Wherever we see this dynamic duo of *Grace* and *Truth* working together, we can safely assume that we are in proximity to Gods Glory. You could say, "Grace + Truth = God's Glory."

One of the reasons so many of our local churches seem to be missing the kind of *glory* that leads to powerful transformation, vibrant worship, and joy-filled service is that they are missing either Grace or Truth, and, in many cases, both. Some *dying* churches have Grace but not Truth, or they will have Grace but harsh facts. Other churches have harsh facts and no Grace. To have the Glory of God, the presence of God that will cause people to come alive, you need both Grace and Truth.

When Grace and Truth come together in a place, pay attention. Glorious things will happen, even in the most broken of situations.

You remember the story of David's sin with Bathsheba, the murder of Uriah, and the subsequent moment of accountability with the prophet, Nathan (2 Samuel 11)? Notice how David's confession is filled with words that point to his encounter with Grace and Truth:

Have mercy upon me, O God,

According to Your lovingkindness;

According to the multitude of Your tender mercies,

Blot out my transgressions.

Wash me thoroughly from my iniquity,

And cleanse me from my sin.

For I acknowledge my transgressions,

And my sin is always before me.

Against You, You only, have I sinned,

And done this evil in Your sight—

That You may be found just when You speak,

And blameless when You judge.

Behold, I was brought forth in iniquity,

And in sin my mother conceived me.

Behold, You desire truth in the inward parts,

And in the hidden part You will make me to know wisdom.

Purge me with hyssop, and I shall be clean;

Wash me, and I shall be whiter than snow.

Make me hear joy and gladness,

That the bones You have broken may rejoice.

Hide Your face from my sins,

And blot out all my iniquities.

Create in me a clean heart, O God,

And renew a steadfast spirit within me.

Do not cast me away from Your presence,

And do not take Your Holy Spirit from me.

Restore to me the joy of Your salvation,

And uphold me by Your generous Spirit.

Then I will teach transgressors Your ways,

And sinners shall be converted to You.

Deliver me from the guilt of bloodshed, O God,

The God of my salvation,

And my tongue shall sing aloud of Your righteousness.

(Psalm 51:1-14)

David's confession is full of Grace and Truth; the Glory of God overtakes him, and his redemption begins.

In Luke's Gospel, Zacchaeus's transformation isn't nearly as well detailed, but it is dramatic. Jesus, that is, Grace and Truth, invites himself to Zacchaeus's home for dinner. By evening's end, Zacchaeus—the tax collector, a man who has been manipulating and stealing from people for a living—makes a statement that reflects his encounter with Divine Glory:

Then Zacchaeus stood and said to the Lord, "Look, Lord, I give half of my goods to the poor; and if I have taken anything from anyone by false accusation, I restore fourfold."

And Jesus said to him, "Today salvation has come to this house, because he also is a son of Abraham; for the Son of Man has come to seek and to save that which was lost." (Luke 19:8-10)

Looking back over my life, I know now that I have looked Glory in the face many times, and what's even more surprising, I have often seen Glory in the most unlikely of places and people, filled with grace and truth.

Conclusion

John's presentation of Jesus as the "Word become flesh" is only one way that Jesus' divinity is expressed in the Gospels, and none of the Gospel writers suggest that they are exhausting the meaning of Jesus' divinity. From John's concept of "The Word become flesh" to Matthew's and Luke's concepts of supernatural birth, the writers point toward his divinity but are humble enough to not feign complete understanding or complete explanation. The Gospel writers were great Christian theologians and teachers because they knew that human beings can never exhaust the meaning of God. They understood, very well, that the most human beings can do when it comes to interpreting the Divine is point toward the Eternal Mystery. Historical attempts to fully define Jesus' divinity over-reach and end up causing more confusion than help. Theological overreaching is one way that human beings create barriers to Jesus' impact in the world. The work of trying to grasp Jesus' God-nature is challenging and it grows the soul, but at the end of the exercise, what we gain is not intellectual information but unfathomable and unsearchable beauty that has the power to transform us in the deepest of ways.

When we try to say more about how the Divine was present in Jesus than can be said or that has been revealed, we end up—even with the best of intentions—putting chains around Jesus' impact. In our futile attempts to bring clarity, we create caricatures of Jesus that mar his image in the world. Let's follow the example of the Gospels. Let's examine and ponder what is revealed and leave the rest as a beautiful mystery that will be imparted by the Holy Spirit.

One of the most beautiful songs I've ever heard comes from the Bethel Music folks. From what I can gather about the song, it originated, spontaneously, during a live worship recording. I think the lyrics capture well where we end up after either an experience of God's presence or an exploration of the New Testament's revelations about God, especially as God is revealed through Jesus. We end with wonder and amazement.

> Wide eyed and mystified
>
> May we be just like a child[6]

6. Amanda Lindsey Cook, "Wonder (Spontaneous)" (Bethel Music, 2014), https://genius.com/Bethel-music-wonder-live-spontaneous-lyrics.

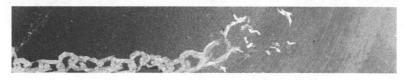

7

HUMAN

What if God was one of us?
Just a slob like one of us?

—*"One of Us"*[1]

Much of the Church-universal is engaged in worshiping the spiritual, divine Jesus. Most, however, miss the obvious; Jesus was a human being. We have to do a lot of heavy theology to explore our belief in Jesus' divinity. His humanity requires, merely, common sense. If we miss his humanity, we will totally miss the blessing of his divinity. His divinity has unfathomable power for us because he was human, fully human.

As Christians, we tend to understand that it takes faith to believe in Jesus' divinity, but because we have so missed the obvious, it now takes faith for Christians to embrace Jesus' humanity. As a dear friend of mine said to me recently, it is more startling for her to hear someone say that Jesus was human than it is to hear to someone say that Jesus is God.

When we focus on Jesus' divinity and minimize or ignore his humanity, we build impediments and barriers to Jesus' influence in the world. I think that, in many instances, there is an intentional strategy to ignore or diminish Jesus' humanity. It is uncomfortable for some of us to observe how Jesus handled certain situations. For example, it can be painful to observe how Jesus treated the marginalized people of his

---

1.   Eric M. Bazilian, "One of Us," Joan Osborne album, *Relish* (Mercury Records, 1995).

community. We would rather worship the invisible, spiritual Jesus than study the behavior of the human Jesus.

Even when we do give due attention to Jesus' humanity, we tend to turn him into a *myth*, by which I mean "an exaggerated or idealized conception of a person or thing." We idealize Jesus' humanity.

Here's an example of what I mean. Michael Jordan has been named by the National Basketball Association as the greatest player of all time. His career ended eighteen years ago in 2003. He was unquestionably an amazing player, almost other-worldly at times, but if you listen to the way some of his most passionate fans talk about him, you would think that he hardly ever lost a game, hardly ever missed a big shot, never lost a playoff series, never had a bad game, and never got outplayed. The more the years pass, the more mythical he becomes. There's no telling what will be said about him twenty-five years from now. In fifty years, he may reach super-human status. The myth that has built up around Jordan is quite contrary to how he describes his career:

> I've missed more than 9,000 shots in my career. I've lost almost 300 games. Twenty-six times I've been trusted to take the game-winning shot and missed. I've failed over and over and over again in my life. And that is why I succeed.[2]

That's a sobering correction to the myth of being a perfect player, isn't it? We could quote hundreds, even thousands, of examples of people and situations that, as time has passed, have taken on mythical dimensions. Think of George Washington, the Founding Fathers, Benjamin Franklin, Harriet Tubman, the Civil War, the Battle of the Alamo, Martin Luther King, Jr., Woodstock, the last natural disaster that hit your area, or even Donald Trump, and he's still current. Because of social media, myths now get created much faster and much sooner; once a myth begins to develop around a person, thing, or event, that myth takes on a life of its own. If there is ambiguity around a person or thing, it only serves to speed up the pace of a myth's development. The fewer facts people know, the more free they feel to fill in the blanks with rumors and the products of their imaginations.

2. "Michael Jordan Quotes." BrainyQuote.com. BrainyMedia Inc, 2022. 6 January 2022. https://www.brainyquote.com/quotes/michael_jordan_127660

My mother-in-law died in 2014. When we, the remaining family members get together, if we talk about my mother-in-law, we don't discuss the details of her life, where she was born, her height, where she lived, how she lived as a black woman, how she made decisions, her core values, the details of her faith, what made her mad, or her spiritual disciplines. We know that they were there and undergirded her life, but seven years after her death, we focus on who she is to us and what she means to us spiritually, emotionally, and relationally. This doesn't mean that the details of her life don't matter. Rather, it means that we know those details, but we focus on treasuring what she *means* to us. We don't say, "Madea (or Mother) was a black Christian woman, a member of John the Baptist Missionary Baptist Church, who served on the hospitality committee, and taught Sunday school where her core teachings were humility, and fear of the Lord." Our conversation are about what she means to us. In many ways, she has become a myth, a beautiful, wonderful myth.

Myths aren't bad. In fact, they are very helpful in giving comfort and hope to people in the shadows of grief. However, if a myth begins to develop around a person whose actual life is important enough to demand our attention and study then we have to make sure that we don't stop with just the idealized perspective of the person.

This is what we have done with the humanity of Jesus of Nazareth. We have created and frozen our mythical imaginations of his humanity. In part, we have done this by over-emphasizing what we view as the divine aspects of his human life.

I want to clarify something before I dig a little deeper. I am not saying that Jesus' divinity is a myth. The previous chapter clearly articulates a thorough conviction that I believe that Jesus was God with us. The myth that we have built about Jesus is not that he is only divine, but that he was barely human. When we envision the humanity of Jesus, he is so heavenly that he ceases to be earthly at all.

Think of some of the depictions of Jesus we have seen over the years. For example, in artistic depictions, Jesus is always looking up at the sky, and is always intense, serious, and somber. In Hollywood presentations of Jesus, his humanity is idealized even more. In these depictions, Jesus seems to float, not walk. He never struggles. He never shows any real emotion. He seems to never get tired, weary, aggravated, or disappointed. He comes across as having only the appearance of being human. His humanity is so sublime that he practically ceases to be human at all. He has become for us a myth. This depiction of Jesus has lodged itself in the collective consciousness of many Christians.

Imagine for a moment if we did the opposite. Suppose we were to minimize Jesus' divinity with an intense anthropomorphism, giving his divinity extreme human characteristics. Think of the thorough humaneness of some of the gods of Greek mythology. They are, basically, human beings with superpowers.

Of course, the Church has, historically, been a major player in the myth created around and about Jesus' humanity. Why has this happened?

In the first five centuries of Christianity, there were numerous internal fights as Christians tried to delineate, distinguish, and define the divine and human dimensions of Jesus. Church councils were convened to work out official doctrines about this matter of Jesus' humanity and divinity. A common theme in the resolutions from these councils was a relentless desire to emphasize the divinity of Jesus.

But the early Church's emphasis on Jesus' divinity begins with Paul, before the councils took place. In Paul's letters, which make up one-third to one-half of the New Testament, Paul makes hardly any mention at all of Jesus' earthly life. It's almost as if Jesus didn't exist for Paul until his supernatural encounter with him on the Damascus Road.

One explanation for Paul's emphasis on the divinity of Jesus might be a matter of timing and proximity. Given that Paul's letters were written very soon after Jesus' earthly life, there would be no need for Paul to spend a lot of time in his letters to account for, explain, or describe Jesus' earthly life. That life had just been completed. His readers knew about Jesus, his disciples, and the stories about them. The oral narratives about Jesus were circulating throughout Paul's world. Writing under the inspiration of the Holy Spirit, Paul focuses instead on the meaning and implications of Jesus' life and ministry.

In Paul's letters, the truth he speaks about Jesus can be misinterpreted and cause people, especially those who are far removed from the actual life of Jesus, to have a mythical perspective of Jesus, over-emphasizing his divinity while his humanity is ignored, downplayed, or idealized.

Let's build a storyline, here. Jesus dies sometime between AD 30–36. His followers begin to spread the story of Jesus throughout Judea and the Roman-Hellenistic world. Because Jesus has just recently lived, there is no urgency for early Christians to record his story. Their focus is on bearing witness and spreading the stories about Jesus to as many people as possible, as Jesus had commanded them to do. As the stories about Jesus spread, local faith communities of Jesus-converts are established by Paul and other apostles. New Christian communities need help in maintaining and sustaining their faith communities. So, around AD 50, Paul and others begin to write letters to local churches to sustain them in the absence of an apostolic leader. There's no great need to explain who Jesus is or give details of Jesus' life to these communities. They are living in chronological proximity to the actual story, and there are stories of Jesus circulating orally among them. What they need help with is understanding: 1) the meaning of Jesus and what his story meant to them, and 2) the practical implications of the Jesus Story for ordering their lives. This is what the books of the New Testament, including the Acts of the Apostles, do. In 1 Thessalonians, you get the added dimension that both Paul and the community to which he writes expect the return of Jesus to happen in their lifetime (1 Thessalonians 4:13–5:11). In such circumstances, it makes sense to give much more emphasis to the Risen Jesus who is soon to return than to the details of Jesus' earthly life.

Fast forward about twenty years, and you have, according to many scholars, the writing of the Gospel of Mark around AD 70. There is a much greater need to give details about Jesus' life in order to: 1) offer more accurate, authority-affirmed accounts of Jesus' life in light of the many oral narratives that were circulating throughout Palestine and beyond, and 2) to keep the memory of Jesus' life alive as the people of his generation were dying and witness about him was spreading to territories that would have been less familiar with, if not totally ignorant of, Jesus' actual life. The writers of the Gospels and their communities began to see the stories of Jesus evolve into distortions and legends, over-emphasizing his divinity while ignoring, downplaying, or idealizing his humanity, and felt a need to provide some correction and balance. The Gospels provide balance to the early Epistles.

To have a comprehensive perspective on Jesus, we need to embrace all of the New Testament as inspired Words of God. However, I suggest that we begin with and measure all things by the canonized records of Jesus' life. In fact, you can't properly interpret the rest of the New Testament unless you first know about Jesus and the life he lived. The theology and practical life instructions of the New Testament's epistles and letters are directly and specifically shaped by the life of Jesus of Nazareth, not just his eternal, divine dimensions, but also his earthly works, his ministry, his miracles, his teachings, and the values he lived out before the world. Jesus' life was not just a casual, pre-event to his coronation as "the King of Kings and Lord of Lords" (Revelation 19:16). Rather, his coronation was directly tied to the life he lived (see Philippians 2:5-11; Acts 2:29-33; Hebrews 12:1-2).

Why is it so important that we take seriously Jesus' humanity and view it in the proper light? It is important because Jesus came to demonstrate the truth about what it means to be human.

I have been pastoring full-time for twenty-five years, and for twenty-three of those years, I served with the thought that I am supposed to help people be good Christians. Now when I look at the Church and the world, I am convinced that God is calling me to help people be good human beings. Jesus came to show us the way to authentic humanity, but we have to pay attention to what he taught us.

Jesus' Project Was Humanity, Not Religion

Jesus wasn't starting a new religion. He wasn't trying to get us to be religious. Jesus was bringing the blessing of Abraham into fruition, that all the people of the earth would be blessed. And what is this blessing? It is many things, but essentially, it is that we, human beings, the crown of God's creation (Psalm 8:5-6), fully become what God created us to become. Somehow, in many sectors of Christian faith, people have come to believe that there's something evil about being human. This is a deep misunderstanding. There is nothing wrong with being human. Human beings were created to be the "image" and "likeness" of God (Genesis 1:26); when we live in alignment with God's design for human beings, we are the crown and glory of God's creation.

I am convinced, when I read the Gospels and the New Testament, that what Jesus is up to is showing us how to be the crown of creation. He's showing us how to live *humanness* as God purposed it. He's showing us humanity at its very best. Furthermore, I believe that to be a Christian is to be engaged in the process and work of becoming fully human. I am a disciple of Jesus because I believe that he is "the way" and "the Truth" about being fully human. Upon what grounds do I make this claim?

"Follow me." That was the invitation Jesus made to those who became his core group of disciples. "Follow me." In responding to that invitation, they left their trades and ways of life and became Jesus' students. What were they learning? How to be religious? How to help administrate the local synagogue? How to preach and teach? How to prepare sacrifices for the Temple? Proper Jewish history? The religious doctrines of Israelite faith? No. At least from what we see in the Gospels, none of these topics were on the *curriculum* for the Jesus School of Discipleship. So, when we read the Gospels, what do see Jesus teaching his disciples to do? He teaches them how to be fully human, not just in the Palestinian-Roman-Hellenistic world, but how to be fully human.

In the Gospel of John, we are told that, near the end of his life, Jesus told his disciples that everything they had seen him do they could do too, and in even greater ways (John 14:12). So, despite how impossible it may have seemed to his disciples that they could fully follow him, Jesus was assuring them that they could live the life that he had lived before them.[3]

As disciples of Jesus today, we too can follow him and learn from him how to be fully human. This is our goal as disciples of Jesus: to follow Jesus and become fully human.

I doubt that I can even begin to communicate the depth of the ways the Church and Christians have missed the mark on this. When I hang out with Christians, attend or participate in Christian gatherings, or engage in activities of local churches, it can be discouraging to see how deeply—by our words and activities—we seem to misunderstand the goal or point of following Jesus.

The goal of being a Christian, of following Jesus, of being Jesus' disciple is *not* to

  – build more church buildings
  – promote American nationalism
  – promote a political party

3.	For a great read on this topic based on John 14:12, see Len Wilson, *Greater Things* (Plano, TX: Invite Press, 2021).

- advocate for a particular social issue
- memorize Bible verses
- go on mission trips
- be safe from life's dangers
- curry divine favor for personal ambitions
- preserve the American way of life
- get rich
- get God to be on our side against our enemies
- carry on family traditions
- become immune to pain and suffering
- make God our "errand runner"
- become super spiritual
- defeat Islamic militants
- overcome a sin or an addiction
- find a spouse
- fight cultural wars
- control your teen's sex drive
- show your gay family members how wrong they are
- receive a miraculous blessing
- be guaranteed a long life
- defeat demons
- develop psychic or extra-sensory perception abilities
- become a preacher
- get a job in the church
- make up for the bad things we've done
- propagate racial or ethnic culture
- organize protest movements
- be happy
- avoid real life

Now, to be clear, some of these things are definite by-products of following Jesus, but it is important to distinguish between things that are outgrowths of discipleship and the goal of discipleship.

I am sure you can think of examples in which people confused a main goal with the by-products of pursuing that goal. Let me offer one of my own. When most kids go to college, they are in pursuit of the goal of obtaining a college degree. In the process of pursuing a degree, however, they might get access to some of the perks of going to college: living in a new city, independence from parents, partying, drinking, pledging a fraternity or sorority, making life-long friends, access to internships, great intramural sports, access to their school's sporting events, access to celebrity professors, and more. However, if any of these side-effects get confused with the main goal of being in college, a lot of time, opportunity, and money can get wasted.

Let's push the college analogy further. Suppose that a high school basketball player from a poor family uses an athletic scholarship to pay for college because he wants to prepare himself for gainful, sustainable employment so he can, eventually, lead his family out of poverty. When he gets to college, he plays well enough that after one year, he becomes a first-round prospect for the NBA draft. If he gets drafted in the first round, he'll sign a multi-million-dollar contract that would allow him to make enough money to provide for his family for two to three generations. There will be people who will counsel him about the importance of having a college degree or the value of the college experience, or the inherent worth of learning, but if his original goal in going to college was to prepare himself for gainful, sustainable employment, so as to lead his family out of poverty, he should enter the draft. Only if he is confused about his main goal would this be a *blurry* decision.

Many Christians and followers of Jesus are deeply confused about the goal of following Jesus. In this case, not only do people get lost in the side-effects, they may not even recognize that true goal. We have to keep asking ourselves, again and again, "What is Jesus trying to do with my life?" Jesus is teaching us how to be fully human, how to be the crown and glory of God's creation. Whatever we do as followers of Jesus, we must never allow anything to become a substitute for this goal.

Unfortunately, church people often learn how to do everything except be fully human. We learn how to fill big sanctuaries with thousands of people. We learn how to make amazing music. We learn how to raise money. We learn how to build organizational structure and culture. We learn how to recruit volunteers and develop leaders. We learn how to study the Bible, pray, and lift up holy hands. We learn how to speak in tongues, create amazing worship slides, and create life-groups. We learn how to do all the things related to the enterprise of Christendom, except being human. Many pastors have learned how to be successful preachers and leaders but have failed at being good human beings. Sometimes, a church gathering can feel like the most un-human place you can be. Church has become something we do, or worse, perform or produce, rather than something we are.

Because the Church is busy performing and producing instead of being human, people can enter our buildings and gatherings and never feel fully alive, which is the real reason why worship attendance, including in the pre-Covid 19 era, has been steadily dropping in America. To put it simply, except for the most committed members, people just don't like "going to church." *Dull, boring, irrelevant, dead* are terms that have been used in my lifetime to describe the Church, so much so, that, if you say those words together, many Americans might immediately assume that you are talking about the Church. The exceptions to this, of course, are the megachurches who are able to spend millions of dollars to create environments that compete with Disney World and Hollywood for their worshipers and for youth and children in their respective areas. With amazing glitz and glamour, these megachurches can make people excited and curious for a while; but, eventually, people get used to the shiny stuff, and they become as uninterested and disengaged as are the people who attend the smaller churches.

I have had the great opportunity to serve in churches of all sizes, kinds, and cultures; they all battled the same disease: a general malaise among members and participants, except for special days or moments. No matter the size, color, location, or theology, that often-spoken-of "80/20" rule held true: 80 percent of the people are surface-participants, and 20 percent of the people carry the church, financially, emotionally, relationally, spiritually, and missionally.

How could this be when the Church is supposed to be chosen, gifted, and empowered by God to address those matters that strike at the very core of what it is to be human? How can a church worship experience be dull and vague when we are in the presence of and engaging with the One who is "from everlasting to everlasting," the One who created us, who knew us before we were conceived, and whose hands knitted us together in our mothers' wombs (see Psalms 90:2; 139; Jeremiah 1:1-5)? If we are dealing in the matters that strike at the very core of people while leading them to engage with the Eternal Creator of their souls, people should "come alive!"

Instead, they come in as "dry bones" and, except for the emotions of the moment, they leave the same, simmering in quiet desperation to find lasting meaning and hope, and trying to figure out how to fight back against the ever-increasing darkness that tugs at their souls. You might even hear people say things like, "There's gotta be more, " or "If I can just get through this week without losing it." They might have just left a church's worship service that included amazing music and a well-put-together sermon or a service that was held in an astonishingly beautiful edifice. Yet they never felt alive. Why? Because despite all the attractive trappings, they never fully engaged their own humanity.

As someone who has been in Christendom all my life, I know what it feels like to sit in a seemingly dynamic worship service and yet be "a thousand miles away" from who I am. I know that feeling, and I know it when I see it on people's faces and in their body language. I see it in discussions on social media.

Human beings, even in our churches, have gotten so lost in doing, producing, and performing *church* that we have forgotten how to be humans.

In fact, in some churches, people are so disdainful of humanity and humanness that the moment you enter their building or gatherings, they try to engage you in extreme religious actions, as if they are trying to get you to run away from your humanness. In such churches, anything that's not overtly religious is suspected of being inappropriate or, worse, demonic. You don't smile. You don't just sit and relax. You don't stay quiet. You don't contemplate. You don't dance unless it is a specific kind of dance that's deemed the "holy dance." In other words, get rid of your humanity.

The inhumanity of the modern church was revealed for me one night while leading a group through a Bible study. A young couple we had never seen before walked in and started engaging in discussions with us. We could tell that the young lady was a *church person*, but the guy with her was not. In his comments, he just spoke truth. He didn't know how to use church language and lingo. It was also obvious that he had some recent, rough life-experiences. At some point in the conversation, we started talking about Jesus' command for his followers to feed the hungry (Matthew 25:31-40). Those of us who were the *church folks* started saying, "If churches would just obey this command and feed the poor, we wouldn't have to worry about our churches being empty. If we would just meet people's tangible needs, we wouldn't be able to build a building large enough to house all the people who would come." The young man who was visiting with us, not being a church person, was visibly bothered by our comments. He looked at us with frustration on his face and said, "What does feeding the poor have to do with growing a church? Have y'all ever been really hungry?"

Somehow, in the midst of *doing* church, we had disconnected Christian ministry from basic human need. Is it even possible for a church that has disconnected itself from a basic human need like food to ever be a resource where people find what Jesus called abundant life? If you can't even empathize with human hunger, how can you empathize with human despair?

Inhumanness is not a phenomenon of the Church alone. It's in our culture at large. What's happening in the Church is probably a matter of secular culture infiltrating the Church. People excel at everything except being human. We know how to be good Republicans, Democrats, liberals, conservatives, pro-lifers, pro-choicers, activists, patriots, Americans, southerners, Californians, Mississippians, architects, engineers, investors, developers, black people, Caucasians, immigrants, natives, politicians, preachers, introverts, extroverts, ENTJs, and ISFPs (Myers-Briggs), 1s and 7s (Enneagram), on and on and on. Yet somehow, we don't know how to be fully human. We can do all these things, yet we seem unable to be able to have a decent conversation with people who are different from us; one of the most popular self-help topics these days is reminding people of the importance of breathing!

We discovered a lot about ourselves and our missing humanity when Covid-19 struck. People were stuck at home, with just their families, and in some cases, just themselves. We realized that we have been so busy, so engaged in performing and producing, that we had missed something about ourselves. With the world shut down, many people rediscovered parts of their humanity. They started looking at and talking with family members. They ate food slower and enjoyed it more, noticing flavors that they hadn't before noticed. They started praying more.

They remembered that it's entirely possible to have a good time with your loved ones without spending hundreds of dollars. They took longer baths. They exercised at home without going to a gym. They called their parents and grandparents and talked to them longer on the phone. They sat on their porches and watched sunrises and sunsets. They noticed the colors of spring and fall. Parents listened to their children's stories, giving them their full attention instead of multitasking. People spent more time reading. They listened more to their favorite music. They reconnected to long-deserted hobbies. A man who owns a restaurant in the French Quarter of New Orleans told me that 2020 was the best year of his life, because he took off from work for the first time in twenty years and spent the year doing what he really loves: drawing and painting. People reconnected with their humanity. They were doing and going as before, but something else happened. They were learning and remembering how to be human.

We are hearing more and more stories of people who are choosing to not return to jobs they hated. I was discussing this matter with someone who said, "I don't get it! Just what are these people going to do?" "Live," I answered, "They are going to Live! They've gotten a 'taste' of their humanity, and they don't want to go back to lives of ceaseless performing and producing while their souls disintegrate." There may be some who are just lazy, of course, but I believe that most of them are refusing to go back to lives that require that they lose their humanity. "Give me my humanity or give me death!"

Jesus, the one who came to give us the ultimate example of full humanity, posed a question to a group of his followers: "What do you benefit if you gain the whole world but lose your own soul?" (Mark 8:36, NLT). Churches quote Jesus on this, but they don't quite know how to use it. We measure buildings, money, tasks, attendance, budgets, accomplishments, achievements, production, and performance because these are tangible and can be easily measured. We don't know how to measure a soul. We don't know how to measure our humanity.

I assert that Jesus is our Way of measuring. Jesus can help us assess and measure our humanity. If we embrace the truth that our goal in being Christians and our goal in following Jesus is to become fully human, and if we call Jesus *Lord*, then we should measure our humanity by Jesus. He is our standard. Connecting our humanity to Jesus will make us come alive!

One of my favorite jazz artists is the late Thelonious Monk. I love Monk because, when I listen to him playing the piano, I can hear him constantly pushing against the boundaries of the jazz, pushing against the boundaries of music, and pushing against the boundaries of how his humanity has been defined. Some of the jazz musicians and historians who were around during Monk's career say that he loved the music he played with his band so much that he would often leave the piano stool, stand up, and dance to his own musical creations. Playing jazz, pushing the boundaries of music and life, made him come alive! There are videos on YouTube of this Monk-phenomenon, and when I see Monk dancing, full-alive, I am more convinced that this is what should happen when a person participates in a church's worship service or ministry gathering. When a church—chosen, gifted, and empowered by God to address those matters that strike at the very core of what it is to be human—leads a community of people to engage with the Creator of their souls, people should come alive!

If churches and Christians became catalysts for people to come alive, to experience and live out the fullness of their humanity, we would be continuing the ministry of Jesus. He modeled, provoked, and curated full human potential. Let's look at some ways he did that.

Fully Human

It is an immeasurable blessing that, instead of a book of rules for how to be human, Jesus gave us himself. There's a kind of *stretchiness* and limitlessness to a story that we don't get from a list of rules. Instead of just telling us to love strangers, Jesus did it, and we get to see the example of what that looks like.

If you read the Gospels looking for religious insight instead of human truth, you might miss Jesus' brilliant example of humanity. I missed it until I read these beautiful words by Max Lucado:

> He was touchable, approachable, reachable. And, what's more, he was ordinary. If he were here today you probably wouldn't notice him as he walked through a shopping mall. He wouldn't turn heads by the clothes he wore or the jewelry he flashed.
>
> "Just call me Jesus," you can almost hear him say.

He was the kind of fellow you'd invite to watch the Rams-Giants game at your house. He'd wrestle on the floor with your kids, doze on your couch, and cook steaks on your grill. He'd laugh at your jokes and tell a few of his own. And when you spoke, he'd listen to you as if he had all the time in eternity.[4]

You don't have to agree with Lucado's description to appreciate his attempt to help us use our imaginations to get a grasp of Jesus' humanity and how beautiful it was.

How tangibly real was Jesus' life? He came from a place from which, it was thought, nothing good could come (John 1:46). Scandal surrounded his birth. In infancy, his family became refugees to protect him from a government's mass killing of male infants of his ethnicity. His society thought he was an *absent-daddy* child. His family and hometown folks thought he was crazy when he started living his purpose. The religious establishment was offended by him. He was deserted by his *homies* at his lowest moments. He was falsely accused of a crime, placed on death row, and suffered a public execution. Yet, despite this very human life, similar to what is experienced by people all over the world, Jesus' story is most often read as almost a religious parable. Christians read his story, gleaning for *spiritual* truths while ignoring the real-life details that can guide us toward a fuller humanity.

Jesus was like all Palestinian Israelites of the first century. Life wasn't segmented into the common and the holy, or the human and the religious. They believed that all of life belonged to God and was lived before God. The Law of Moses contained rules for everything from what to eat to how to make sacrifices for sin. So, we should read the Gospels and Jesus' story through this lens. The Jesus-model of humanity is to treat all dimensions of life as spiritual. To grow as a human being is to grow spiritually. If God is pleased with you as human being, God is pleased with you spiritually. This is the definitive characteristic of Jesus' humanity; he saw the goal of life as striving to live one's whole life as an expression of God's will (Matthew 6:9-10).

According to Jesus, to be fully human is to:

— center one's entire life in God through prayer, intimate fellowship with God, and obedience to God's will (see Mat-

4.   Max Lucado, *God Came Near* (Portland, OR: Multnomah Press, 1987), 54.

thew 6:9, 14:23; Mark 12:29; Luke 6:12; 18:1).

- live in community with others (Matthew 6:9-10; 9:1-8; Mark 1:14-15).

- live with mission and purpose (Mark 1:14-15; Luke 4:16-21; 19:10).

- refuse to compromise one's identity and purpose for convenience (Luke 4:1-4).

- live free of the need to prove one's value or worth to others (Luke 4:9-13).

- learn to live by God's timing and God's design (Luke 4:5-8; John 11).

- refuse to *sell* one's soul for success, wealth, power, fame, or the avoidance of suffering (Luke 4:5-8).

- accept suffering as necessary for human growth (Mark 8:34; Luke 22:39-46).

- face and overcome one's fears (Matthew 10:28; 14:22-33; John 11).

- value people over laws and systems (Mark 2:27).

- live with a readiness to acknowledge sin, confess, and repent (Mark 1:14-15; Luke 18:9-14).

- not be attached to things, including material wealth (Matthew 6:19-34; 19:16-30).

- forgive (Matthew 5:23-24; 6:14-15; John 20:21-23).

- love others, including strangers and enemies, by sacrificially serving their needs, their potential, and their divine purpose (Matthew 5:38-48; 25:31-46; Mark 10:42-45; 12:31; Luke 10:25-37; John 5:1-9; 13:1-5).

- love oneself (Mark 12:31).

- nurture one's spirit to be bigger than outward circumstances (Mark 4:35-41).

- trust others (Jesus trusted his disciples with his mission during and after his life on earth.)

- strive to live one's life as God's Word in the flesh (John

1:14; 5:19-20).

- build your life on things that have eternal value (Matthew 6:25-34; 7:24-27).

- empathize and show compassion for others in their suffering (Matthew 9:35-38).

- practice humility as a way of life (Matthew 18:2-5; Luke 14:7-35; John 13:1-5).

- live under yokes (structures of discipline) that produce a quality life (Matthew 11:25-30).

- relentlessly, see and value the humanity of people, ALL people (Mark 1:40-45; Luke 7:36-50; 13:10-17; 19:1-10; 23:32-43; John 5:1-9).

- overcome the dread of death (Matthew 10:28; 16:21-28; John 11).

- learn to be okay with ambiguity and uncertainty (Matthew 14:22-33; John 11).

- live by faith (Matthew 17:20; Mark 4:35-41; 9:23).

- learn to live beyond social and cultural boundaries (Matthew 15:21-28).

- don't let the opinion of people and crowds determine how you live your life (Matthew 15:39; Luke 5:16).

- be careful about how you treat children (Matthew 18:2-10).

We could go on, but these are some of the basic lessons Jesus gives us about living fully human lives. What's new is that, instead of seeing these things as a set of religious rules, I am asserting that we need to see them as lessons on authentic humanity. In fact, these lessons will make a lot more sense to us if we stop *religionizing* them and see them for what they are, that is, Jesus teaching us how to live authentic, human lives. To live by these guidelines is to become God's original design for human beings, the crown and glory of God's creation.

"But I thought that Jesus and Christianity are about the cross of Calvary!" The unchaining of our lives from *religionizing* means that we will have to break the habit of seeing Jesus only as the one who died on the cross for our personal sins. Jesus' crucifixion does, of course, have ultimate significance for us for many reasons. The Gospels are clear that the crucifixion was the apex of Jesus' life and ministry. However, the Gospels are also clear that Jesus' entire life has significance for us. How could it not when Jesus was the very Word (expression, thought, will) of God in human flesh?

Everything about Jesus of Nazareth matters. A faith system that includes everything about Jesus is entirely different from a faith system that is built exclusively around and upon the cross.

That second version helps explain why some people view Christianity as being only about personal sin, personal salvation, going to heaven after you die, and having absolutely nothing to with how we live our lives, socially and communally. These Christians probably feel that it wouldn't hurt to imitate Jesus' life, but at the end of the day, the only thing that matters is that you pray this prayer:

> "I confess that Jesus Christ is Lord. I believe in Jesus' death for me. I repent of my personal sins. I give my heart to Jesus so I can go to heaven when I die."

In this perverted version of traditional Christianity, salvation is a transactional matter, unrelated to who we are becoming as people. Add to this: 1) a very limited understanding of salvation as, basically, "having a ticket" for heaven; 2) a perverted understanding of grace as something that relieves us of the responsibility of having to actually do anything to participate in our salvation; and 3) the doctrine that, once you've done the salvation transaction, you are saved forever, no matter what. The natural consequence is the Christianity we have seen, unfortunately, throughout Church history. In this version of Christianity, people can participate in and perpetrate all kinds of evil in the name of Jesus and wearing the name of Jesus, without conscience or accountability, especially if, as they do evil, they are convincing millions of other people to do the Jesus transaction.

The missionaries of this version of Christianity, for example, often show up in foreign lands, dehumanize and murder the natives, and then boast about bringing Jesus to that land and converting thousands to Christianity.

This version of Christianity is a profound perversion of everything for which Jesus lived, taught, and died! In fact, it stands in opposition to everything for which Jesus lived, taught, and died. In this behavior, these *Christians* have become enemies of the cross (Philippians 3:18).

There is absolutely nothing wrong with cross-focused Christianity or the prayer of salvation. The problem occurs when these things get separated from a more holistic embrace and practice of Christianity that is connected to the life that Jesus lived as a human being.

This perversion of Christianity can be combatted when we stop separating the cross from the rest of Jesus' life. Jesus of the cross is an extension and coronation of the Jesus who touched lepers, defended the weak, and taught us to value all people, even strangers and our enemies. The more serious we are about the cross, the more determined we should be to strive to follow Jesus in living authentic human lives.

May the Holy Spirit unchain our hearts to love all of Jesus. May we surrender to the full work of the Holy Spirit so that, as we are nurtured to love and worship the Risen Jesus, we will also submit to the work of the Holy Spirit in reproducing Jesus' beautifully lived life, Jesus through us.

Jesus, you are beautiful in all your ways.

PART II

JESUS: THE CHAIN BREAKER

8
MISSION

Despite how often Christian apologists try to argue that Adolf Hitler is an example of the evil caused by atheism and secularism, the truth is that Hitler often proclaimed his own Christianity, how much he valued Christianity, how important Christianity was to his life, and even how much he was personally inspired by Jesus - his "Lord and Savior." There is plenty of evidence that he was critical of Christian churches for seeking independence from the state, but his vision of "Positive Christianity" was significant to him.

—Austin Cline[1]

What's Wrong with/in the World?

We have already considered that Jesus came to reveal God to us and that he was the "Word of God" living among us as a human being. We have also considered that Jesus came to show us God's picture of being fully human. Jesus had to come to do these things because there was something wrong with the world. All Christians agree that our world is broken, and that Jesus was sent by God to fix whatever is wrong, but we vary widely in what we see as the problem with our

---

1. Austin Cline, "Adolf Hitler on Christianity: Quotes," *Learn Religions* (June 25, 2019), https://www.learnreligions.com/adolf-hitler-on-christianity-quotes-248190.

world. We might all agree to call it *sin*, but how we define sin varies widely as well.

I suggest that one of the main reasons we so easily chain Jesus to inhumane and wicked agendas is that we are often unclear about what exactly is the problem Jesus came to fix. Church history is littered with incidents of human atrocities committed in the name of Jesus.

Consider again the quotation at the beginning of this chapter. Adolph Hitler would not be such a perplexing character of history if, as Austin Cline points out, he had been an atheist. Instead, Hitler claimed Christianity as his faith and claimed Jesus as his Lord. As he made his claim on Jesus, he and his loyal Nazi supporters went on to murder some 11 million human beings (6 million Jews and 5 million non-Jews) until they were eventually defeated by the allied forces that opposed them. Jesus was claimed by Hitler and the Nazis with the support of a large segment of the Church in Germany, both Protestant and Catholic, and suppressed beneath a mountain of Nazi nationalism, patriotism, unbridled lust for power, and raw racial ethnic hatred. The truth is that Jesus was claimed by Hitler and the Nazis so that he would not, through the faith and witness of his true disciples, be a threat to Nazi power and the Nazi agenda.

What happened in Germany under Hitler was not an isolated phenomenon in human history since the incarnation. Just to be clear, what I am talking about here is not just that Christians have done and do bad things. Rather, I am referring to the times when Christians have committed unimaginable atrocities in the name of Jesus and as "banner carriers" for the Christian faith. I am excluding atrocities committed by single individuals who profess to be Christians. Those can easily be dismissed by some people as acts of mental illness or singular insanity. The atrocities I refer to are those committed by large groups of Christians in the name of Jesus in a way that represents a shared worldview, a shared theology, and a shared understanding of Jesus' message and ministry.

Jesus' name has been used to cover up many atrocities:

- The Crusades (1096–1271), horrible atrocities committed against Muslims and Jews
- Rhineland Massacre of 1906 and the Libson Massacre of 1506

- Genocide of Native Americans in North and South America

- North Atlantic slave trade and chattel slavery in North America

- sexual abuse of children by Catholic priests, with almost no accountability

- lynchings by white mobs in America

- Ku Klux Klan's widespread, murderous terror against Black Americans from the early to mid-twentieth century

- the suppression of women's rights and full citizenship in America

- the January 6, 2021 attack on the American Capitol

. . . just to name a few.

My point here is not to beat up on Christianity. Religious-based human atrocities are definitely not exclusive to Christians. However, my criticism of a religion's evils should be of my own, the faith that I claim, the faith that shapes my life and that I try to live and share.

I am not saying that theology or doctrine are the singular causes for these atrocities. In fact, we know that many of these acts of horror were driven by economic, political, and other factors, as well. However, I am calling out the way that the perpetrators of these atrocities justified and validated their actions with their version of Christian theology and their interpretations of the message and mission of Jesus.

I once saw a picture of a KKK gathering in a church with a huge sign hanging on the wall behind the group of Klan members that said, "Jesus Saves." It is an unforgettable image, especially if you are an American and, even more, if you are an African American. People can debate the meaning of words, but a picture that captures the commitment, worldview, and theology of a group of people is irrefutable. Take a look:

The power of this picture for me is that it displays the way a mindset or a social initiative that is vehemently opposed to the life, message, and mission of Jesus can become a deeply ingrained, entrenched way of life. It has happened, and it still happens, always with the most horrendous consequences.

It is, therefore, of ultimate importance to Christians that we struggle as best we can to have the right understanding of Jesus' message and mission. The dangers in getting it wrong are tremendous. When people have the wrong understanding of Jesus and his mission, the consequences are unimaginably horrible. So many times, when people distort the mission and message of Jesus, people die, the influence of the Church is severely damaged, and the image of Jesus becomes connected to issues and agendas that are vehemently opposed to who he really is. Maybe, if we can better grasp Jesus, his mission, and his message, we can prevent evildoers from perverting his name and his purpose in the world. At least, Christians ought to understand Jesus' mission and message well enough to know when something is fundamentally opposed to it. The seeming inability of Christians to discern false versions of Jesus' mission today has a lot to do with our own, apparent, ignorance of his mission.

Interpreting Jesus' Mission Through the Biblical Story

What did Jesus think was wrong with the world, and what did he think God sent him to do about it? Matthew 1:21 says that Jesus came to "save His people from their sins." In Luke 19:10, Jesus defined his mission as to "seek and save that which is lost." On a different occasion, Luke tells us this story to explain Jesus' mission:

> So He came to Nazareth, where He had been brought up. And as His custom was, He went into the synagogue on the Sabbath day, and stood up to read. And He was handed the book of the prophet Isaiah. And when He had opened the book, He found the place where it was written:
>
> > "The Spirit of the LORD is upon Me,
> >
> > Because He has anointed Me
> >
> > To preach the gospel to the poor;
> >
> > He has sent Me to heal the brokenhearted,
> >
> > To proclaim liberty to the captives
> >
> > And recovery of sight to the blind,
> >
> > To set at liberty those who are oppressed;
> >
> > To proclaim the acceptable year of the LORD."
>
> Then He closed the book, and gave it back to the attendant and sat down. And the eyes of all who were in the synagogue were fixed on Him. And He began to say to them, "Today this Scripture is fulfilled in your hearing." (Luke 4:16-22)

I want to place these statements about Jesus' mission within the context of the whole story of the Bible.

Have you ever really read the Bible? I mean, have you fully read it, and not just read it for quick answers, instantaneous comfort, helpful information, or, for preachers, a sermon? I no longer assume that people have read the Bible thoroughly, because I am so shocked at how few people know the comprehensive story that the Bible tells. And when people don't know the story that the Bible is telling, then they will *use* the Bible for singular—and often very selfish—agendas and purposes that end with extreme misinterpretations of biblical passages. This is how our misinterpretations of Jesus begin.

The Bible's story begins in a garden (Eden) and ends with a city (the new Jerusalem). Actually, it begins with "God created the heavens and the earth," and between Genesis 1:1 and Genesis 1:2 it feels like a galaxy's worth of space. Verse 2, if you are paying attention, is startling. What God creates is in a state of chaos. The Hebrew phrase for it is "*tohu wa-bohu*" (*tohu vavohu*), which means, "formless void."[2] *Tohu wa-bohu* is, I believe, an early indication of what the Bible is trying to say overall about the problem of creation. Yet God, through God's Word, speaks order, purpose, and community into creation; then God creates human beings, bearing God's image, and brings us into community with the rest of creation, as Creation's managers and cultivators (Genesis 1:26-30). Creation has shifted from being *tohu wa-bohu* to, in God's assessment, to being *tov me'od*, "very good" but not perfect. Creation is a beautiful community that human beings are to cultivate and develop to fulfill God's will and purpose, there is also space (freedom) not to yield to God's design. Enter Adam and Eve.

Adam and Eve were living in community with God and creation, but they made a choice that broke that community. They were then alienated from each other, from God, and finally, from creation as a whole (Genesis 3), and from that point forward, the Bible's story is about God's work of restoration. It's the story of God restoring creation to God's original plan and purpose. The choosing of Abraham and the Israelites, the promises established with Abraham for the sake of all people, the deliverance of the Israelites from Egyptian slavery, the giving of the Law, the stories of Israel's charismatic judges, the prophets, the establishment of the Davidic kingdom, the journey of the presence of God, the ark of the covenant, the building of the Temple, the exile and restoration, the rebuilding of the Temple, the coming of John the Baptist and Jesus, the life and ministry of Jesus, the Crucifixion, the Resurrection, the coming of the Holy Spirit upon the Church, the ministries of the disciples and Paul (the book of Acts): all are about this one theme, God restoring creation to God's order, purpose, and community . . . with added dimensions! We know this because, by the time the story

---

2. Walter Brueggemann, Terence E. Fretheim, and Walter C. Kaiser, *The New Interpreter's Bible: Genesis to Leviticus* (Nashville: Abingdon, 1994), 342.

ends, we have, not a garden, but a city. The New Jerusalem is the culmination of God's work of creating and restoring.[3]

Now, notice that overcoming sin is a major theme in the Bible story, but it isn't the main point of the story. The main point of the story is that God desires a creation with human beings as its crown, yielding to God's purpose, and dwelling in community with one another and with the divine community ("let us make . . .," Genesis 1:26).

Next, notice that God's restoration is not just about or for human beings. We ended the last chapter resolved to get the root of our struggle to be fully human, but the whole story of the Bible places the failures of our humanity and Jesus' work to help us within the broader context of God's all-inclusive work of restoring all of creation. Biblically speaking, it's just not correct to think of God's work and plan of salvation as about people only. Moreover, based upon Genesis 1:26-31, it seems that God doesn't have a definition or vision of full humanity that doesn't include the proper management of the rest of creation. Jesus came to do something about human beings doing something about everything!

Notice that the Bible's story is not primarily about a personal, individual, spiritual salvation. It's a story about all of creation existing and responding to God, together, inclusive of individual responsibilities. Even if salvation begins personally and individually, if it's the faith of Jesus and faith in Jesus, that salvation is meant to spread into every corner, community, and crevice of creation.

When we miss God's purpose for us, the result is broken community. This is the essential problem with human beings and with all of creation. And if community is broken, relationships are broken. Jesus talked about community and relationships in nearly everything he taught. Even when Jesus addresses other issues, he is almost always relating everything to relationship: relationship with God, with others, or even with ourselves.

The actions of Adam and Eve after they commit sin are telling. They feel deep guilt. They become acutely self-conscious. They feel shame. They stop seeing themselves at one with each other and creation, and they begin to try to hide from and blame each other and God.

---

3. For a fuller exploration of the Bible's story, I highly recommend N. T. Wright, *Simply Christian*, (New York: HarperOne, 2009).

In his letter to the Romans, Paul says that physical creation is suffering the *fallout* of creation missing its purpose and existing in broken relationships.

> I consider that our present sufferings are not worth comparing with the glory that will be revealed in us. For the creation waits in eager expectation for the children of God to be revealed. For the creation was subjected to frustration, not by its own choice, but by the will of the one who subjected it, in hope that the creation itself will be liberated from its bondage to decay and brought into the freedom and glory of the children of God.
>
> We know that the whole creation has been groaning as in the pains of childbirth right up to the present time. Not only so, but we ourselves, who have the firstfruits of the Spirit, groan inwardly as we wait eagerly for our adoption to sonship, the redemption of our bodies. (Romans 8:18-23, NIV)

As the community of God's creation is broken and alienated, the effects filter down and out and manifest as misery that we experience every day in our personal and social lives. Racial hatred, sexism, neglect of the aged, the abiding disgust some people feel toward their physical self-image, the mistrust between spouses, and psychosis, which is, literally, a break from shared reality; all of these things are the fallout of creation having missed its purpose and, as a result, being mired in guilt, shame, blame, and hiding.

Let me mention two other things that are crucial to a correct understanding of the Bible's view of what's wrong with us and the rest of creation. First, we must include in our diagnosis that, in the Bible's story, there is a community of beings, specified in the Gospels as satan and demons, who are opposed to God and God's creation. I prefer to use the word *evil* to refer to this opposition to God's plan for creation, and the word *sin* to refer to things we do to participate in and cooperate with evil. Sin is what evil uses to destroy relationships and community. There are forces and powers at work in creation working to destroy community and prevent creation from existing in community with God and to the glory of God. As the crown of creation, human beings are free to choose to live in rebellion to God's will for creation, and there are some *things* who are glad to help us rebel.

Second, we must acknowledge a theme that runs throughout the Bible, probably because, in some way, it strikes at the heart of what has gone wrong with human beings. Human beings are extremely prone to *idolatry*, which is, essentially, giving to ourselves, things, or people the place in our lives and world that belongs only to God. The Bible implies that idolatry is a common avenue through which the forces of evil bring attacks against creation, and that idolatry defiles and deforms creation (e.g., Paul's words in Romans 1). Human beings were created with drive to worship, and when we worship something other than God, it disturbs our spiritual well-being and the spiritual atmosphere around us in ways that we can't quite fully understand. Paul says that idolatry deforms human character as nothing else does (Romans 1:25-32). Being a pastor for a long time, I have seen firsthand the devastating effects of idolatry. People's countenance, their emotions, and their misery after an idol crashes—which they always do—is one of the saddest things to ever witness. I have stood at the bedsides of dying people. I have watched families grieve from the pain of losing a loved one. I have sat with couples and listened to the language of diminished love and passion. Yet nothing has been sadder to me than the despair of a person whose idol has failed him or her.

Now, let's revisit Jesus' mission and mission statements through the lens of the Bible's story, and compare Jesus' mission to the behavior of people who call themselves *Christians* in the world today.

Jesus' Mission Was to Be a Blessing

As an Israelite, Jesus saw himself as the fulfillment of the covenant with Abraham. He came forth from a people who believed that, through them, God was going to bless all people. From the picture of Jesus that we are given in the Gospels, Jesus embraced this heritage and promise passionately. In fact, at no point in the Gospels do we see Jesus using power, privilege, and resources for himself. In every scene of his life, he uses his resources for the sake of others to heal, to restore, to recover, to encourage, to guide, to inform, to empower, to be a blessing. As Jesus' followers, we inherit the legacy of the covenant with Abraham, and we should see our ourselves as "blessed to be a blessing."

Yet this is not what we see from most people, especially in America, who call themselves Christians. We act as if God, faith, and life are all about what we get or what comes to us. What we see from Christians is a sense of entitlement; we see a claim to privilege; we see an addiction to power, and we see an unwillingness to suffer, let alone to suffer for others.

Some Christians come across as spoiled when they interpret people disagreeing with them as persecution.

Churches admire and exalt the privileged, the wealthy, the famous, and the powerful. In fact, the more privileged, wealthy, famous, and powerful people are, the more the Church admires, reveres, and exalts them. Churches disciple people to help grow the church and make the name of the Church great instead of helping them grow the Kingdom and make great the name of the Lord. Any member who doesn't conform is given less care, less attention, and less inclusion in the life of the faith community. We measure pastors and leaders by their wealth, status, fame, and power; often, we measure these things without reference or attention to their character or their service to others. "Prosperity gospel" preachers twist the message of Jesus and the entire Bible to somehow mean that the point of the life of faith is to build wealth and avoid suffering. Churches take from the poor and disenfranchised to enrich the rich and powerful celebrities of Christendom. In black communities all across America, you can find instances where church memberships, church buildings, church budgets, pastors' salaries, and church egos get bigger and bigger, while the quality of life for the citizens in those communities diminishes more and more. Churches use guilt, shame, and fear to manipulate people to become good servants to the kingdom of the local church. Church members behave like fans who participate in their local church only when it's convenient and demand that every sermon and every song be catered to meet their individual needs.

Contrary to the one whom they claim to follow, the one who gave up power, privilege, and status to serve, many Christians see the distinctive mark of authentic faith as an invitation to obtain and hold on to power, privilege, and status while growing the number of people who serve them.

Right now, in America, there are people who profess Christianity who refuse to take the pre-cautionary measure of wearing a mask to help protect others from a deadly virus that has already killed nearly 1 million Americans! And what reason do most of these people give for not wearing masks? They say that it infringes on their right and freedom to choose how they want to live, and many of them say that Jesus is on their side in refusing to do a simple thing that might help to save people's lives.

Right now, in America, there are people who profess Christianity as they abort unborn babies, without conscience, in order to protect their status, their reputation, or their comfort. Many of these persons are folks who criticize their political enemies for their lack of attention to social justice, but when it comes to abortion, they become champions of private, personal, and individual choice.

Many Christians twist Scripture to make the Bible a foundation for self-promotion, self-centeredness, self-indulgence, and self-worship. You can often read social media posts with statements like the following, typed onto beautifully colored backgrounds with a cross in the middle:

- Get rid of anybody who doesn't make you feel good.

- Block the people who disagree with you.

- If you can't help me achieve my goals, I'm removing you from my life.

- If you're not making a contribution to my life, I don't want you in my life.

- Stop hanging out with people who don't see your value.

All of these statements encourage and express a mindset that places oneself at the center of reality. Everything and everybody is measured by his or her ego and self-interests, "in the name of Jesus."

Too many Christians have become the takers, not the givers, of society. In this version of Christianity, Jesus came to help each person achieve wealth, power, fame, and self-fulfillment, and if Jesus isn't helping with these things, he's rejected as being irrelevant.

On the contrary, Jesus saw his mission as a continuation of God fulfilling God's promise to bless "all the families of the earth" (Genesis 12:3). He says of himself, "the Son of Man did not come to be served, but to serve, and to give His life a ransom for many" (Matthew 20:28). Beneath all the ways that Jesus lived out his mission as the Messiah was this basic, essential mission: to serve and be a blessing to and for the world.

Jesus' Mission Was to Restore Broken Creation

Jesus saw himself as a savior of the broken realm that God, the creator of the world, wants to restore. This is contrary to the belief prevalent among many progressive Christians that human beings are basically good, and that, if we can just be set free from guilt, shame, and *shoulds*, we will guide the world to get better and better. We struggle to be fully human, the crown of God's creation. There is a lot of good in human beings, but there is also an overwhelming tendency toward evil. This tendency must not only be taken into account; it should be taken seriously. Jesus took it seriously. God took it seriously. Part of the meaning of Jesus' crucifixion is that it points to the presence and power of evil in people and the world.

According to the Bible and Jesus' mission, our physical creation is not perfect and self-sustaining. From the very beginning of the story in which Jesus lives his life, the physical world is good, but not perfect, and it requires human management and cultivation. Yet, a lot of the opposition to efforts to care for the climate and the natural world comes from people who present themselves as Bible-believing, Jesus-following Christians. Many of these people take the biblical assertion that human beings are the "crown" of creation to mean that the natural, physical world has value only as a servant to human beings, but in Genesis 1–2, human beings are just as much the servants of the physical world. We exist together in a mutual relationship of life-giving service. Maybe this is what Paul meant when he wrote, "God was in Christ reconciling the world to Himself"(2 Corinthians 5:19), and that the rest of creation is waiting for human beings to become who God created us to be (see Romans 8:19-22).

We betray Jesus when we, bearing Jesus' name, present a view of the world as perfect and without need for transformation. Jesus came to be the light in a world he perceived to be filled with darkness. He came to bring "the gospel" (good news, Mark 1:14-15) to a world that, in his view, is filled with bad news. Jesus came to lead his followers in storming the gates of hell (Matthew 16:18-19). In some ways, hell has set up camp in God's creation. In a world that's perfect, that just needs to be left alone and allowed to continue making steady progress toward perfection, and where human beings are good and naturally evolving toward a higher morality and a higher humanity, there is no need to

- preach good news to the poor
- heal the brokenhearted
- liberate captives
- help the blind to recover their sight
- liberate the oppressed

In one of my favorite movies, *The Lord of the Rings: Fellowship of the Ring*, Frodo's closest and most loyal friend Sam says to him that there is some good in this world, and it's worth fighting for. Yes! There's good in this world, and we have to fight for it, because there are forces at work in the world that oppose the good. Jesus believed this, and he came to fight for the good in the world. If we are true to him, we will join the fight.

Jesus Came to Save Us from Sin

Jesus came to save us from our sins, says Matthew 1:21, but what is meant by *sin*? The Bible presents us with a much broader view of sin than a simple list of bad things that we do. The Bible views sin as a social problem as much as a personal, individual problem. The Bible views sin as things we fail to do as much as things we do wrong. The Bible views sin as having multiple dimensions. Sin has a pull. It has a power. It is a state of being. It is an act of disobedience to God's will. It is "missing the mark" of what God has purposed for us, and it has consequences. According to the Gospels and the rest of the New Testament, Jesus' mission was to address the problem of sin in all its manifestations. Jesus saves us from sin in all the ways it affects us.

Jesus seemed to be most concerned about sin as "missing the mark" of God's purpose for us. Jesus came from a people who had seen the devastating consequences of missing God's mark for them. In one of the saddest moments in the New Testament, we see Jesus sitting in the hills surrounding Jerusalem, weeping over the city and its people, because they have missed God's purpose. Because of this, Jesus foresees impending, disastrous consequences.

The main way we "miss the mark" as human beings is in our failure to be fully human, the crown of God's creation. Human beings have drifted so far away from the mark of God's purpose for us that God determined to give us a living, tangible model. In showing us who we have the potential to be, Jesus saves us from our blindness to who we really are. He unchains us from all the perverted models of humanity that we have seen, learned, and experienced since we were children. If we are the crown of creation, the key to God's work of restoring all of creation is to help us live into the fullness of who we were created to be.

Yet the Church has turned Christianity into a morality tale rather than a comprehensive way of living under the love and purpose of our Creator. Following Jesus gets turned into, "Stop doing bad things so you can go to heaven when you die." We limit sin to a personal matter, and we ignore its social dimensions. Some segments of the Church believe Jesus will save us from the consequences of sin, but they ignore his power to save us from the pull and power of sin. Being *saved* gets defined as being saved *from* something but not *for* something. In this misinterpretation of Jesus, sin is anything on a list that your culture has defined as being bad. The typical sin-list includes adultery, fornication, lying, stealing, cursing, and homosexuality. Culture says that, if you can manage to not do any of these things or not get caught doing any of these things, you can prove that you're a faithful disciple of Jesus and that you're definitely going to heaven.

When Christianity gets presented as a *morality club*, there are a few consequences that follow: 1) We create hypocrites, because, when your participation in a group is determined by your ability to be perfect in following the rules, everyone hides, because no one is perfect. 2) The set rules are always rules that are chosen by the status quo and the powers-that-be. The rules aren't for the rulers of the group. Rather, they are chosen to protect the rulers and control the ruled. This is one of the ways that slave masters controlled their slaves in America. They created a strict moral code, by which they themselves did not abide, and they called it Christianity. In order for the slaves to hope to make it to heaven, they had to abide by "Christ's commands," or rather, the slave masters' moral code. 3) We create injustices, because, in such a system, the only people who get caught and are held accountable are the weakest and most disenfranchised people, those who don't have the resources—power, relationships, or influence—to be able to hide their sins or keep people from blowing the whistle on them. 4) Illegitimate guilt and shame are multiplied and magnified. 5) Instead of people developing a healthy "fear" (holy reverence) for God, they live in fear of being exposed. 6) We redirect people's attention from following Jesus to following rules. The former brings life. The latter creates misery, fear, guilt, shame, and death. 7) Instead of people learning and growing as human beings, they learn how to keep rules, at best, or hide their failure to keep the rules.

A person can obey all the rules and still miss the mark of who God has called human beings to be (Luke 15:1-32; 18:18-23).

I once saw a Tik-Tok video made by a young adult in which he was pretending to be God, sitting in heaven, looking down on creation. In the first scene, God looks down and sees the oppression of black slaves and is unmoved, as if to say, "no big deal." In the second scene, God sees a young black man using foul language, gets upset, and unleashes a fatal lightning strike on the young man. The video demonstrates the insanity of the version of Christianity that's not rooted in the Bible and in the perspective of Jesus.

The resurrected, unchained Jesus responds to and handles sin quite differently from these distortions of the Church. For Jesus, sin is personal and social, inward and outward. For Jesus, overcoming sin is just the beginning of being fully human. For Jesus, what matters more than trying to be perfect in keeping all the rules is to learn how to overcome the failures and continue one's growth toward full humanity. In fact, when I read the Gospels, I can see that Jesus put his disciples in situations in which they were doomed to fail, so that they could learn how to trust in something greater—and better—than their ability to be perfect in keeping the rules. For Jesus, sin is good provocation to pray. Finally, Jesus lived with confidence that sin does not and will not have the last word about human beings and creation (Luke 22:31-34). In his view and in the view of the Bible, sin is never bigger than the forgiveness and grace of God (Matthew 6:9-15).

Jesus Came to Seek and Save the Lost

When we read, in the context of the whole story of the Bible, that Jesus came to seek and save the lost, we know it means that Jesus restores people who have been lost and alienated from God's creation community. Jesus came to redeem and restore all of creation, but he focused on "the lost." It is amazing how easily and consistently the Church forgets this aspect of Jesus' mission. As a result, we surrender Jesus to the control of the wealthy, the powerful, the status quo, the insiders, and the enfranchised of the Church. We treat our local churches like exclusive private clubs, and we focus our resources on pleasing the *insiders* instead of being a blessing to all within our reach, especially, those who are *outsiders* to our church.

The Church in America is an enfranchised entity. We belong to the status quo, and in most cases, we barely know how to serve and relate to outsiders, especially people who are severely challenged, physically, economically, emotionally, socially, and mentally.

A few years, ago, in a conversation with a bishop of The United Methodist Church, I was reminded of just how exclusive local churches have become. He was expressing his concern about local churches in minority communities being prepared to serve the large numbers of men who would return to those communities. He said to me, "Most churches that give attention to incarcerated persons serve these persons while they are incarcerated, but from what I can see, they are not prepared to welcome those people into their churches." I knew his words were true, at least for me. I had been serving as a full-time pastor for twenty years. I had gone into prisons to *minister* to incarcerated persons. I had raised money for prison ministries. What I had never done was lead a church I was serving to welcome ex-incarcerated persons. For sure, I've had plenty of ex-incarcerated persons in local churches that I served, but for the most part, these persons had been out of prison and had found their way back into a stable, status-quo lifestyle. As I talked to the bishop that day, I started thinking to myself that I don't even know if I would be comfortable around someone who has just come out of prison. How could this be? How can a minister and follower of Jesus Christ hesitate to connect with and relate to ex-incarcerated people? This is what happens when we disconnect the Church from the mission of Jesus. This is what happens when we pander to the insiders of the Church. This is what happens when we forget that Jesus came to reclaim people who have been edged out of human community. And if we forget this, then we will not prepare and equip ourselves to serve marginalized people. We'll just keep on trying to excel in serving people who are already in our churches.

Don't these words of Jesus penetrate our hearts about people who are on the outside of our churches?

> What do you think? If a man owns a hundred sheep, and one of them wanders away, will he not leave the ninety-nine on the hills and go to look for the one that wandered off? And if he finds it, truly I tell you, he is happier about that one sheep than about the ninety-nine that did not wander off. (Matthew 18:12-14, NIV)

Jesus' mission to the lost is another opportunity to remind ourselves that God's work of restoration targets more than our souls. The *lost* are not just those who are spiritually lost, as many have interpreted these words of Jesus to mean. In the Gospels, "the lost" are those Israelites who have, for one reason or another, been relegated to the borders of Israelite faith in the belief in that they had been rejected by God. Tax collectors, the sick, lepers, the blind, the demon-possessed: these people were excluded from participation in the full life of Israelite faith. Jesus, however, says he came to reclaim and restore them. Jesus' "reclamation project" has a social dimension that is no less significant than the personal, spiritual dimension.

Jesus, carrying the heart of God in his bosom, was showing the world the radical, inclusive love of God, and if he decided to hang out with someone or give someone a moment to make a request for healing, then he was saying to the world, "God loves this person, too!" Jesus could have given his time to anyone, but he opted to spend time with this person. Over and over again, Jesus opted for the lost, those who were the *untouchables* of his society.

Jesus knew how affirming such a moment of being chosen could be for people. God did it for him at his baptism. As Jesus came up out of the water, the Holy Spirit, in the form of a dove, descended upon him, and those gathered heard God's voice saying "This is my beloved Son, in whom I am well pleased" (Matthew 3:17; also see Mark 1:11; Luke 3:22).

As a theology student at the age of twenty-six, I was serving as an intern at Mount Vernon United Methodist Church in Houston, TX. Dr. Zan Holmes, a preaching icon of the African American pulpit and an icon of The United Methodist Church, came to preach. When he stood up to preach, he called my name and said to the congregation, "You are blessed to have him here. Watch him. Keep your eyes on him." I can't even put into words what I felt in that moment. Zan Holmes had given me his affirmation, right in the presence of the people who, in that phase of my life, meant so much to me. This is what Jesus did for the most excluded people in community. Claiming divine authority, Jesus said to the lost: you are mine; you belong; you are a son/daughter of Abraham (Luke 13:10-17; 19:1-10)!

This preference to help social and religious untouchables is part of the reason Jesus runs afoul of the Israelite power structure and ends up on the cross. He was upsetting the status quo by redefining who's in and who's out; the only people he seemed to say were *out* were those who acted as if they were the only ones who were *in*. Nothing made Jesus angrier than when people used religious power to make others feel excluded, rejected, and oppressed (see Matthew 23).

Depending on the context, any one of us could be the "lost," or the outsider, and it is good to know that in every such situation, Jesus shows up and gives preference to the "lost."

Conclusion

Jesus came to be a blessing, not to take, but to give. Jesus came to be a tool of God for God's work of restoring all of creation. Jesus came to save us from "missing the mark" of God's purpose for creation. Jesus came to save us from anything that opposes, impedes, or distracts us from God's plan to have a creation with human beings as its crown, yielding to God's purpose, and dwelling in community with one another and with God. And Jesus came to seek and save the lost.

People do a lot of things under the name of Jesus, but if we are going to say to the world that we are acting as Jesus in the world, then our actions should be consistent with Jesus' mission and actions. We don't have to commit a holocaust to misrepresent Jesus, and we don't have to participate in a slave trade to make an idol out of Jesus. We can betray Jesus any time that we act in the world under his name in a way that is inconsistent with Jesus and his mission.

9
MESSAGE

I think hell is something you carry around with you. Not
somewhere you go.

— Neil Gaiman , Sandman: Season of Mists[1]

In the last chapter, we began to grasp what Jesus saw as being wrong with the world and what God sent him to do about it. We looked at Jesus' mission statement. Now let's look at his message. His message is just as revealing about how Jesus saw the world as his mission statement. So, what was Jesus' message? First, let me tell you some things that are *not* his message.

If you took a poll, today, and asked one hundred people, "What was Jesus' core message?" you would probably get one of four different kinds of answers.

1) You might get answers that are very general or that reflect a very casual attitude toward the Bible, such as,

- be kind and do the right thing;
- don't do bad things, like using foul language, drinking, or abusing children;
- don't break the rules;
- be responsible, work hard, and keep your promises; or

---

1. Neil Gaiman. AZQuotes.com, Wind and Fly LTD, 2022. https://www.az-quotes.com/quote/594887, accessed January 06, 2022.

- all religions serve the same God.

2) You may also get answers that reflect some knowledge of the Bible but are not related specifically to Jesus, such as,

- pay your tithes and go to church;
- let justice roll down like waters and righteousness as a mighty stream;
- trust God;
- obey the 10 commandments;
- read the Bible and try your best to obey everything in it; or
- hate the devil and don't let him use you to do evil.

3) Or you may get answers that are connected to Jesus but aren't his core message, such as,

- help the poor, the homeless, the sick, and those in prison;
- people should pray about everything;
- forgive others and forgive yourself;
- change your ways and live right;
- have faith;
- do great things for God;
- love one another.

4) Or you might get the church-answer, which purports that the message of Jesus says you must "confess that you are a sinner, repent from your sins, believe that Jesus died for your sins, accept Jesus as your personal savior, get baptized, and you will be saved from hell and go to heaven."

Most of these answers are good things, and I don't deny their value and truth. However, none of them is the primary message that Jesus proclaimed in his ministry.

Most Christians probably couldn't tell you: 1) what it means to be a Christian, 2) the central claim of the Christian faith, 3) how Jesus defined his mission, or 4) Jesus' core message. For most people who call themselves Christians, being a Christian means, basically, "I'm religious. I believe there's a God. I believe that God loves me. Jesus died for me, so I don't need to feel guilty about anything. I'm pretty sure that I'll go to heaven after I die." That's the essence of what most people mean when they say they are Christians. Add to that some special elements to fit different cultural contexts—be against abortion, help the poor, fight injustice, or learn to speak in tongues—and you have Christianity in North America, in the twenty-first century. The label *Christian* has become a catch-all for *religion*, except for religions like witchcraft or satanic worship. This is why people who decide to become serious about their spirituality or serious about being followers of Jesus often flee from the label of *Christian*. Christianity, as a whole and as a collective witness in the world, is mired in chaos. If we called all Christians in the United States to participate in a true, national day of prayer, we would be hard-pressed to come up with a list of prayer concerns that reflect a shared ethos, value system, or way of seeing current events. America is deeply, vehemently divided, and the Church can't help heal the divisions because each faction has its own, unique version of Christianity that's radically different from the others in content or in practice. Christianity could change the world if we could just decide who we are.

Jesus came proclaiming good news. What was the "good news" (gospel) that Jesus proclaimed?

> After John was put in prison, Jesus went into Galilee, proclaiming the good news of God. "The time has come," he said. "The kingdom of God has come near. Repent and believe the good news!" (Mark 1:14-15, NIV)

"The kingdom of God has come near." That's the good news that Jesus proclaimed, and that's the message that most of his parables and teachings help to explain.

Everything about Jesus—his identity, his divinity, his humanity, his mission, his crucifixion, his resurrection, his commission to his followers, the Holy Spirit's presence within and among believers, the ongoing mission of the Church that Jesus founded—must all be understood in relationship to the Kingdom of God. Without understanding what

Jesus meant by the Kingdom of God, his ministry may be severely distorted and misinterpreted.

Addressing Some Key Questions

How have so many people become true disciples of Jesus without ever believing that Jesus' core message is the Kingdom of God? I, for one, do not subscribe to the belief that our relationship to God is determined by our intellectual knowledge, so, please, do not take this insight to imply that you can't be *saved* without knowing this. To think this way is to imply that anyone who doesn't have the capacity to grasp certain ideas intellectually is without hope for salvation and relationship with God. I *do* believe, deeply, that we are saved by grace, which means that God does for us what we can't do for ourselves, and God helps to do what we find it hard to do. God knows our hearts, and God can see when a heart is turned toward God in surrender (see, e.g., 1 Samuel 16:7; Psalm 44:21; Proverbs 21:2; Jeremiah 17:10; Hebrews 4:12). If God waited for us to know and understand enough about God before *saving* us, none of us would ever be *saved*.

The tragedy of being *saved* but not knowing about the Kingdom is that this ignorance prevents us from experiencing the abundance of the Kingdom, and it causes us to misrepresent Jesus to the world. This is like a man pledging a fraternity but not getting involved and staying connected. This man will, eventually, misrepresent that fraternity, and he will miss the many benefits that come from being a member of a worldwide, mutually enriching community of people.

Do pastors, priests, and preachers not know this? How can they not know what Jesus' core message is? My guess is that many pastors don't know this because, as is true for all of us, we read with preconceived notions and built-in filters, so we tend to see in the Bible what we already believe, unless we take the step of reading with intention, consciousness, and awareness. First, many pastors, priests, and preachers are simply sharing what they already believed before they tried to teach or preach from a particular biblical passage. Second, most pastors, priests, and preachers haven't been trained in how to interpret the Bible appropriately. Third, and most important, I think that many pastors, priests, and preachers know this, but choose to ignore it because the message about the Kingdom is disruptive to the Church enterprise. The message about the Kingdom would disrupt most of how we *do* church. Priorities and values would change. Budgets would change. Worship services would change. How we measure the effectiveness of local churches would change. How we choose and measure leadership would change. How we treat people would change. It would change what and how we preach (can a Black preacher *whoop* about the Kingdom as the close of a sermon? lol). Changing all these things would disrupt the economic systems and social structures of the Church, and most church-folks *ain't* about to let the message about the Kingdom mess with their money and their status.

But I thought that heaven was a place to go after we die? A lot of Christians have believed, and still believe, this lie. Jesus said that the Kingdom of God is "at hand," "near", available to us, right now. In another passage, Jesus said that the Kingdom was present wherever his disciples were carrying out his mission under his assignment and authority (Luke 10:1-9). Certainly, there is more of the Kingdom to come, but we can begin to experience it and live it here and now through our relationship with Jesus in the Holy Spirit.

Think for a moment of all the oppression and abuse that the Church, in history, has perpetrated against people—with those people's permission and submission—by dangling the hope for heaven after death before them, and then telling them that the way to make it into heaven was to become a Christian and obey Christianity's rules. The rules were, of course, a selective set of rules, picked out of the Bible by the perpetrators, which could be used to control the victims and suppress any desires for a better life on earth.

So, for example, during the ordeal of the chattel enslavement of Black people in America, two of the most highlighted Scriptures were, "Slaves, obey your earthly masters with respect and fear, and with sincerity of heart, just as you would obey Christ" (Ephesians 6:5, NIV); and "Slaves, obey your earthly masters in everything; and do it, not only when their eye is on you and to curry their favor, but with sincerity of heart and reverence for the Lord" (Colossians 3:22, NIV).

It's a miracle that Black people were able to see through this manipulation, enough, to fight for their liberation and, eventually, full citizenship in America. They must have paid attention to the fact that, as they were being told to just survive on earth and prepare to go to heaven after they die, their slave masters were relentlessly building *heavens* for themselves on earth. I hope this book will help get the word out that exchanging lands and other resources for the hope of heaven after death is not a "good deal" and is not a deal with which Jesus agrees. In fact, I submit to you that Jesus and the Kingdom of God are vehemently opposed to such an idea, and that this idea is a manifestation of the evil kingdom that Jesus came to overthrow and overcome.

Let's dig into what Jesus meant by his core message: "the Kingdom of God is near!"

Why a Kingdom?

As an Israelite, Jesus saw the world through the lens of kingdoms. The people of his day, his fellows Israelites and others would have heard his announcement of a new kingdom as attention-demanding news. For his fellow Israelites, it provoked their hopes for the coming of the Messiah who would re-establish the Davidic monarchy. For others, his announcement would have had any one of numerous, wide-ranging responses, from fear and concern to hope and curiosity. However, while Jesus was using a concept with which they were familiar, he meant something far bigger and far more important than just the coming of a new, human kingdom.

We discussed, in the previous chapter, that the story of the Bible is the story of how the creation community was broken by sin, and that Jesus saw himself as being sent by God to help heal it. We saw that the Bible's story is the story of God at work in the world, restoring the creation community to what God purposed it to be. If we are true to Jesus in how we interpret his core message, then his core message means, in part, that the Kingdom of God is the restoration of a community— God's creation community.

A kingdom is a community. It is a community of people brought together by a shared and defining reality, a reality that, because of how it defines the community, becomes the authority for that community. A community can be determined and defined by location, blood, an educational institution, a building, a disease, an income level, an experience, a fear, a hope, a sports team, a nationality, a political party, a political issue, or a god, just to give a few examples. The shared, determining, and defining reality of a community is in a sense the *king* of that community. One's participation in that community is determined by one's loyalty to that determining and defining reality. For example, you would not be able to continue to participate in a community of people brought together by their shared value of hating bike riders if you start to espouse the view that people who ride bikes are wonderful people. Of course, people belong to multiple communities, and the authority of the community to which a person is most loyal is that person's ultimate reality and god.

Let's be clear: Jesus values individuals. The Bible is clear about this truth. However, Jesus, the Israelites, and the God they worshiped, saw the world—and all reality—through the lens of communities (kingdoms). God loves each one of us individually, and because God loves us, God calls us into full humanity and full participation in the whole of God's creation community.

This is definitely different from the viewpoint of people since the Enlightenment, particularly in the Western world. In the West, and especially in the United States, individualism rules. By individualism, I mean seeing reality through the lens of individuality instead of community. Individualism measures everything by how it affects us individually. In America, our heroes are individuals who have experienced astounding, solo success. We celebrate the people who "pull themselves up by their own bootstraps." It's the American way. In America, it is believed that you, the individual, can achieve anything that you set your mind to achieve. The pinnacle of American life for most Americans is to make the cover of *Time Magazine* in celebration of exceptional, individual success. Rugged and relentless individualism is at the heart of all our favorite national myths, from Paul Revere to Barack Obama.

This focus and high value placed on individualism has infiltrated our understanding and interpretation of the Christian faith. Being *saved*, being a Christian, came to be defined by a focus on individualism. Being a Christian has come to be about having a personal relationship with Jesus Christ, individual morality, individual purpose, and the individual soul going to heaven after death. In this version of Christianity, there is often some value given to community. In fact, most churches that present the message of Jesus as being primarily about individual salvation are surprisingly vigorous supporters of life-groups (community) as the vehicle through which people get discipled into mature believers.

9

I think that they understand and embrace the communal nature of the Kingdom, but they find it difficult to get people's attention with anything but a message about what God is going to do for people personally and individually.

The truth is that, just as some churches preach individual salvation but revel in community behind the scenes, all claims of individualism are deceptions. No one "pulls himself up by his own bootstraps." Every successful person has been helped along the way by a community of individuals and groups of people. The person who claims to have made it alone is, either, lying, ungrateful, an amnesiac, or doesn't know help when it appears. It's impossible to exist in this world without being sustained by some aspects of community. Your life is shared, nurtured, supported, and enhanced by other people. You are living on *borrowed* resources. You probably didn't make the clothes you have on. You are in a building that you probably didn't build; if you did build it, the resources and knowledge to build it came to you from others. You can relax in some degree of safety because of others, near and far, who place their lives on the line to keep you safe. If you have driven a vehicle today, the road or streets your drove on, the laws that provide for safe driving, the fuel that fueled vehicle, and the vehicle were all provided for you by others. The oxygen that fuels your body and your very life are not things of your own making. They were given to you. You are a product of community.

Years ago, Martin Luther King, Jr., said, "We are caught in an inescapable network of mutuality, tied in a single garment of destiny. Whatever affects one directly, affects all indirectly."[2]

Jesus' response to Dr. King's words is, no doubt, "Exactly!" This is the view of reality that Jesus was "carrying in his bosom" when he came with his good news. Jesus saw the world—God's creation—as a community, but it was broken, distorted, and undermined. Let me paraphrase Jesus: "The right time has come. The Kingdom is here! God is restoring all things! God's creation community is coming back together!" What many of his fellow Israelites misunderstood about this message was that this kingdom Jesus proclaimed is not just another kingdom that would compete with the other earthly kingdoms. Jesus' Kingdom was not just *a kingdom*. Rather, it is *THE Kingdom*, the Kingdom above all other

2. Martin Luther King, Jr., *Why We Can't Wait*, (Boston, Beacon Press. 2011), 87, Kindle

kingdoms. It is the community that God created at the beginning, being restored and evolved!

If Jesus' core message is the coming of the Kingdom of God, then, as we bear witness to Jesus in the world, we must recognize him not merely as personal Savior and Lord. We must present him as the Gospels present him, and as God sent him, as the savior and lord of the entire creation community. He is the shared, determining, and defining reality and authority around which all of creation is destined to gather. No one has an exclusive claim on Jesus. Not even a faithful local church that is passionately serving as outpost or mission station of the Kingdom can claim Jesus as its own. Jesus is the Word—through whom all of Creation came into being—made flesh, and he is the One sent by God to launch the full restoration of Creation. Jesus isn't just a personal savior, he's a— if you're ready for it—community developer!

Let's look deeper into the meaning and nature of the Kingdom that Jesus proclaimed as the good news that the world desperately needs.

The Kingdom of God and the Anti-Kingdom

The Gospels present Jesus as launching (restoring) a community that comes into conflict with powers and forces in the world that are opposed to Jesus' community and all that it represents. Immediately, after he was baptized, *satan* met him in the desert in an effort to distract, divert, and disengage Jesus from his work of restoration. As soon as his ministry began, the signs of this anti-kingdom started showing. Illness, disease, and suffering were everywhere. Demons were screaming and shrieking in irritation just from Jesus' presence. Mark records that Jesus' first healing miracle was an exorcism of a demon that had possessed a man and was crying out through the man:

> "Let *us* alone! What have we to do with You, Jesus of Nazareth? Did You come to destroy us? I know who You are—the Holy One of God!" (Mark 1:23-27)

And that's just the beginning of the opposition that Jesus encounters.

Luke tells us that, after Jesus overcomes the devil's temptations in the wilderness, "the devil . . . departed from him until an opportune time" (Luke 4:13). This seems to set up the understanding that what happens later in Jesus' life (his crucifixion) is caused by the devil and the community of evil forces that are opposed to Jesus and his purpose.

The way demonic forces are described in the Gospels indicates that they are organized into a *kingdom* (community), because they: 1) seem to abide by rules, 2) they refer to themselves and act as a group, and 3) they understand and show respect for authority (Mark 5:1-13). The Gospels are saying that it's not just that there is evil in the world, but this evil is organized, structured, purposeful, and powerful. It's organized opposition to the Kingdom Jesus proclaimed. It's organized darkness. It's a group of entities that have come together around a determining and defining reality and authority: to oppose God's Kingdom. Evil exists and functions as a community.

The Gospels indicate that, while the forces of this organized opposition can attack, tempt, influence, deform, denigrate, aggravate, distract, divert, oppose, infiltrate, and possess human beings, they don't and can't ultimately control our freedom to choose how we will live. They tempt us in our decision-making, influence our decision-making, and give energy and power to our bad decisions, but they are not ultimately responsible for our decisions (Matthew 16:22-23; Luke 4:1-13; 22:3-6, 31; John 8:44; 12:31-32; 13:2).

Furthermore, the Gospels tell us that, while these forces can cause illness (Luke 4:39; 5:13; 13:11-16), and while they do seek to destroy individuals, these forces have a much bigger plan in mind than just our individual destruction.

These forces were irritated by the presence of Jesus because, like any established kingdom, they were not willing to give up their claim of rule and authority. These forces knew that Jesus had come to usher in God's Kingdom and usher out the kingdom of evil. As this conflict happens, we choose whether we are going to live under the rule of the Kingdom that Jesus was ushering in or the kingdom of evil. Heaven and hell are not just post-death realities. Both are here with us, available and functioning right now. Right now, you can either go to heaven or you can go to hell.[3]

This is a good place to note something important about the kingdom of darkness. Progressives and intellectuals have done a great dis-

---

3. For a provocative exploration of how our choices can place us in a heaven or hell, see: Arthur Jones, *Solid Souls* (Plano: Invite Press, 2021).

service to the ministry and impact of Jesus in the world by casually dismissing *talk* about satan, the devil, and demons as ancient superstition or ignorance resulting from a pre-scientific understanding of nature, biology, and disease. We don't have to agree on how to understand this dimension of life. We will not all understand it the same way. Yet we should all take this dimension of reality seriously. If we don't, then we will not prepare ourselves or the people we are discipling to live victoriously in the face of structured, organized evil, in whatever forms it may present itself. If we don't take this dimension of reality seriously, then we keep people "in the dark" about the One who has overcome the kingdom of darkness.

There are segments of the Church, however, that make too much of the devil and demons, so much so, that they blame every bad thing on demons and place no responsibility on human beings for the choices they make that bring suffering and disaster. These misguided Christians give so much hype to the devil and demons that the evil forces take *center stage* in church services purposed for the worship of God. I was once a part of a local church that was headed down a path of a kind of glorification of the devil, meaning the devil was getting far too much attention in our worship services and special gatherings. Thanks be to God that a guest preacher came along; when he saw what was happening, he addressed this in his very first sermon preached in that church. "Let me make this very clear," he said. "I serve a big God and I know there is a little devil, and I'm not going to spend my time worried about the devil. Why are you running from the devil when you ought to be chasing after God!" When he spoke those words that night to people who had been deeply concerned with the dangerous direction in which the church had been going, the emotional release sounded like an explosion. Chains of fear, bad theology, religious abuse, shame, and religious intimidation were falling off of people that night.

The dark forces in this world, however we may conceive of them, are real. They are armed against our humanity, our relationships, creation, and God's Kingdom. They must be taken seriously, so that we can learn to guard and war against them. However, we should never make them so big in our minds, hearts, churches, and worldviews that they consume our attention.

Captives of Hell

Again, like the Kingdom of God, hell is a community. The defining and determining reality is opposition to God's new community, the Kingdom of God. The forces of evil are its citizens, but human beings can become its captives. Like Egypt when it enslaved the Israelites, hell is an enslaving community. It enslaves, dehumanizes, and destroys human life, human potential, and human capacity. It wars against all of creation, but it targets the crown of God's creation. The phrase, "a living hell" is not far from the truth. "Living hell" is hell on this side of death. But how do people become captives of "hell on earth," the "living hell"?

People can become captives of hell when they make bad choices that take them into devastating consequences. People can become captives of hell when they develop a character-deforming, spiritually debilitating habit that keeps them locked in a cycle of misery. People can become captives of hell when they live in inhumane conditions for an extended time. People can become captives of hell when they have "burned the bridges" of all their relationships and have no one remaining who is willing to help them with their problems. People can become captives of hell when they carry the deep wounds of horrid experiences, such as, rape, child molestation, or long-term mental, physical, sexual, or spiritual abuse. People can become captives of hell when they experience a psychotic break from the shared reality of their community. People can become captives of hell through long-term hunger, homelessness, or deep poverty. People can become captives of hell by the bad choices of other people against them (the Pharoah who came to power and who "did not know Joseph" made choices that put the Israelites into "living hell"). People can become captives of hell through sustained, deeply ingrained idolatry (worship an idol and a demon will appear). People can become captives of hell by making heart-covenants with things that result from immoral or unethical situations. I could go on, but my point here is not to be exhaustive of all the ways that people can enter "hell on earth." I give this list because it comes by way of my experiences as a pastor, friend, father, husband, brother, son, partner, colleague, and counselor. I have witnessed firsthand the circumstances that make people captives of the forces of darkness. By the way, notice my use of words. I say that these things can make people captives of hell. People can also experience tragedies and temptations in their lives and not only reject hell but become inspired to live heroic, exemplary lives. Some people who have difficult experiences become motivated to begin an *all-in* pursuit of the Kingdom that turns their lives into light.

What makes the difference? Why do the same experiences send some people spiraling into "living hell" and send others exceling into the Kingdom of God? The difference is hope. Everyone, at some point, experiences profound pain or suffering of some sort, in one way or another. What turns that pain into hell is hopelessness or despair. One way that I like to define hell is "misery without hope." This is why it makes sense to say that, in one sense, hell is not so much a place; hell is "something you carry around with you," because despair—misery without hope—is, indeed, a status of a person's soul that is with its captive, everywhere he or she goes. I am sure you have seen people wrapped in the throes of misery. Such people are, and are in, "a living hell."

I have seen hell many times in my life. Not the eternally burning fire that some Christians believe will be the eternal existence of some people, but I have seen "hell on earth." I have heard its sound. I have smelled it's revolting stench. Misery without hope is manifest all over our world.

I once heard the sound of hell—misery without hope—at the funeral of a teen. A highly touted football player, he was in his final year of high school and had just been offered a scholarship to play football at the University of Oklahoma. After a silly argument with his best friend over a dog, his friend grabbed a gun, shot, and killed him. On the day of the funeral, I walked into the sanctuary that had a seating capacity of 1,200. It was packed with high-school students. At the beginning of the funeral, a football highlight video of the boy was shown with the song, "It's So Hard to Say Goodbye," by Boyz II Men. It was a profoundly sad moment and, as you might imagine, the students started crying. But this wasn't just crying. What I heard that day was something other than crying. The sound I heard was wailing. The sound I heard was the sound of broken spirits. What I heard that day was misery without hope. I heard the sound of hell, which had gathered in the sanctuary of a church and was trying to take captive a bunch of kids who were facing a sadness and sorrow that they didn't have the spiritual capacity to overcome.

As I sat and waited to do the eulogy, it was so clear to me what that moment demanded of me. No matter what I had planned to say, what I had to do was bring hope. That was twenty-three years ago, and I don't think that I have ever had more clarity and conviction in a moment leading up to preaching than I had that day. I knew I had to face down hell and bring hope that is Jesus into that moment.

I have seen hell in neighborhoods that were so ravaged by poverty, crime, and pain that misery had set in and turned those neighborhoods into mission stations of hell. There are no limits to how destructive and dark human behavior can be when people are devoid of hope. Maya Angelou once described what it's like to see a neighborhood wrapped in misery: "In my twenties in San Francisco I became a sophisticate and an acting agnostic. It wasn't that I had stopped believing in God; it's just that God didn't seem to be around the neighborhoods I frequented."[4]

When Jesus came as "the Word made flesh," he saw hell too. On one occasion, the sight of it seemed to nearly overwhelm him, and it provoked him to make an explicit call for help in his mission to bring to hope people bound in misery.

> Jesus went through all the towns and villages, teaching in their synagogues, proclaiming the good news of the kingdom and healing every disease and sickness. When he saw the crowds, he had compassion on them, because they were harassed and helpless, like sheep without a shepherd. Then he said to his disciples, "The harvest is plentiful but the workers are few. Ask the Lord of the harvest, therefore, to send out workers into his harvest field." (Matthew 9:35-38, NIV)

Jesus saw people in hell, and he gave them hope. In a sense, a very basic, simple definition of the Kingdom and its purpose is *hope*. The Kingdom of God is hope. It brings an end to people's unending despair. The Kingdom doesn't protect us from pain and moments of misery, but it does keep us from being driven by our pain into "hell on earth," because the Kingdom is hope. That's the first reason it is good news!

Later in his ministry, in answer to his own prayer, Jesus makes a big announcement about the addition of a new branch of God's restoration project. Those who trust and follow Jesus will become a part of a new sub-community of the Kingdom, a mission-station of God's work to restore broken creation, a community of people who are "prisoners of hope":

4.   Maya Angelou, *Wouldn't Take Nothing for My Journey Now* (New York: Bantam Books, 1994), 74, Kindle.

And I say also unto thee, That thou art Peter, and upon this rock I will build my church; and the gates of hell shall not prevail against it.

And I will give unto thee the keys of the kingdom of heaven: and whatsoever thou shalt bind on earth shall be bound in heaven: and whatsoever thou shalt loose on earth shall be loosed in heaven (Matthew 16:18-19, KJV).

Jesus' message was twofold. He proclaimed the good news about the Kingdom of God and the good news about the destruction of the evil kingdom that had taken people and Creation captive. The Church was founded by Jesus to help and continue his work of proclaiming the good news and "storming the gates" of hell to release its captives.

Conclusion

Jesus shows up in our lives in many ways. He meets us where we are. He doesn't wait for us to understand him correctly or reach a certain level of maturity. Each person who follows Jesus sees the core message of Jesus as being the truth that opened up his or her life to Jesus. In the Missionary Baptist churches in which I worshiped and learned about Jesus as a child, I doubt that most of those people, including the preachers and pastors, were aware that Jesus' core message was, "the Kingdom of God is here." Jesus met them in their place of need with grace and truth, and their experience of him shaped what they said about him to others. So, in those churches, they would say things like, Jesus is

- bread when I'm hungry.
- water when I'm thirsty.
- my lawyer in the courtroom.
- my doctor in a sickroom.
- way-maker.
- heart-fixer.
- mind-regulator.
- healer.
- faithful friend.

- – wonderful counselor.
- – provider.

Their experience of Jesus in their moments of need came to shape and define their understanding of Jesus' message and mission. I dare not say that they were wrong. Whatever understanding of Jesus' message that you may have of Jesus' message and mission should be held on to and treated as sacred, so long as your understanding doesn't contradict what we know about Jesus and the Kingdom. It is urgent, however, that you do one thing: measure and manage your understanding of Jesus' message by this core message: "The kingdom of God has come near. Repent and believe the good news!" Otherwise, we will, unintentionally, become barriers to the blessing of Jesus being experienced by all of creation.

Let's look, now, at the nature of life in God's new community.

10
NEW LIFE!

Our goal is to create a beloved community and this will require a qualitative change in our souls as well as a quantitative change in our lives.

—*Martin Luther King, Jr.*[1]

Christians were never meant to be normal. We've always been holy troublemakers, we've always been creators of uncertainty, agents of a dimension that's incompatible with the status quo; we do not accept the world as it is, but we insist on the world becoming the way that God wants it to be. And the Kingdom of God is different from the patterns of this world.

—*Jacques Ellul*[2]

I have tried drugs and a little of everything else, and there is nothing in the world more soul-satisfying than having the kingdom of God building inside you and growing.

—*Johnny Cash*[3]

1. The Power of We. Interfaith Mission Service. Quotes section https://www.interfaithmissionservice.org/about-us/vision-and-mission/beloved-community-resources/

2. Matt Chamber,. (2012, December 16). *Holy Troublemakers.* Church Leaders. https://churchleaders.com/pastors/pastor-articles/164280-matt-chambers-to-day-agree-anarchist.html

3. Suman Varandani. (2018, February 26). *Johnny Cash Quotes: Lyrics To*

Because I believe in Jesus' good news, and because I have seen the power of community, I say that, when people need help, no matter what condition they are in, the quickest and most effective way to help them is to get them connected to a healthy community, a community that is healthy in the thing that has broken them. When Christianity truly works, when it leads to deep, substantive, and ongoing transformation and growth toward maturity, it's because it excels in providing community. This is not to deny the power of God to miraculously effect change in a person's heart, but if that miraculous moment isn't followed up with connection to healthy community, the blessing will eventually be lost. The Kingdom, God's New Community, is a spiritual reality but a tangible, practical truth. Community works. It especially works when it is sustained by the life of Jesus and presence of Jesus.

What did Jesus teach and demonstrate about life in God's New Community?

HOPE

Hope makes us strong even if our circumstances don't change. I will never forget the night I stood at the bedside of a loyal church member as she was dying. We had been praying with her for two years, that God would heal her, but it was not to be so. She had asked for her closest friends and family to come to her. We were there, in the room together, gathered around her bed. As you might imagine, we were all broken and in tears, but not her. Through her oxygen mask, I saw the biggest, most beautiful smile I've ever seen. After engaging with each person, she called for me, her pastor, and asked for a piece of paper and a pen. On the paper, she sketched out the shell for her funeral service. There was one song: "Mercy Said No," a song recorded by the amazing music artist, CeCe Winans:

> When sin demanded justice for my soul
> Mercy said no[4]

Remember Songwriter On His 86th Birthday. International Business Times. https://www.ibtimes.com/johnny-cash-quotes-lyrics-remember-songwriter-his-86th-birth-day-2657540

4.   Greg Long, Don Koch, David Allen Clark, "Mercy Said No" lyrics © Warner Chappell Music, Inc, Universal Music Publishing Group. You can hear to CeCe Winans's recording of it. here: https://www.youtube.com/watch?v=JQaOl7qH31w

Even in the grips of physical death, she was full of hope and overcame despair. As I stood at her bedside, I saw . . . Heaven, the Kingdom, God's New Community. I saw Jesus living through her.

I am very clear about this: authentic witness to Jesus is, always, a catalyst for hope. Make no mistake about it. And in the darkest of situations, our ministry of hope can be the difference in keeping people from giving in to despair. Every local church needs a team of people in whom the Holy Spirit has nurtured the gift of being able to "hew stones of hope out of mountains of despair!"[5]

Repentance and Humility

When Jesus started his ministry and announced God's good news about the Kingdom, he called for a certain kind of response to the news. We are to repent: change and believe (Mark 1:14-15). At another point during his ministry, Jesus said that humility was required.

> And he said: "Truly I tell you, unless you change and become like little children, you will never enter the kingdom of heaven. Therefore, whoever takes the lowly position of this child is the greatest in the kingdom of heaven." (Matthew 18:3-4, NIV)

We see a similar quote in John 3:3 (NIV):

> Jesus replied, "Very truly I tell you, no one can see the kingdom of God unless they are born again."

Jesus is saying, literally, that unless we humble ourselves and re-pent—change or turn away from what we know and think is right and start over as beginners in learning how to live—we will block ourselves from experiencing and participating in God's new community.

The teamwork of repentance and humility is how we enter into and maintain our citizenship in the New Community. However, they are required as more than *entrance passes* into the community; they become the foundational disposition of the community's citizens. We can be described as people who live in humility with a readiness to repent. Hu-mility with a willingness to repent (change) is like magic in relationships

---

5. Adapted from the inscription on the Martin Luther King, Jr. Memorial in Washington, DC.

and communities. To get a better grasp of this truth, imagine for a moment, a community in which the opposite happens. Imagine a community in which every person is an arrogant, self-righteous, prideful, never-yielding, self-serving, know-it-all. Maybe you've been in a community that you would describe that way. Such a community would be a colony of hell on earth, and such a community would eventually destroy itself.

Pain, brokenness, and mourning are often the ushers of entry into the Kingdom, because they tend to produce the humility and willingness to repent that are necessary to enter the Kingdom. Maybe this is why Jesus said:

> "Blessed are the poor in spirit, for theirs is the kingdom of heaven.
>
> Blessed are those who mourn, for they will be comforted.
>
> Blessed are the meek, for they will inherit the earth."
> (Matthew 5:3-5, NRSV)

After being forced by the prophet Nathan to come to terms with his sins, David, in his powerful prayer of confession and repentance, said:

> The sacrifice you desire is a broken spirit.
>
> You will not reject a broken and repentant heart, O God.
> (Psalm 51:17, NLT)

In Psalm 119:71, we see a similar disposition:

> My suffering was good for me,
>
> for it taught me to pay attention to your decrees. (NLT)

We should seek, however, to live in such a way that we don't have to suffer and be humbled by affliction. We can choose to "walk humbly with [our] God" (Micah 6:8) and to remain willing to repent (change) as God directs. What do we mean by humility and repentance?

Humility is hard to define. I like Merriam-Webster's attempt at it: "freedom from pride or arrogance."[6] Humility is the willingness to give up or restrain power. Humility is choosing to place restraints on the impulse to assert one's rights, privileges, authority, and power in relation to another person. Humility is not feeling the need to prove yourself. It is safe to say that the collective witness of the Bible is that the Bible

---

6. Merriam-Webster, s.v. "humility," accessed December 15, 2021, https://www.merriam-webster.com/dictionary/humility

places a premium on humility as an ingredient in building healthy relationships and healthy communities. Heather King, in her blog, *Room to Breathe*, gives us an excellent list of the Bible references to humility.[7] Her list includes the following passages (all from the ESV):

- "If my people who are called by my name humble themselves, and pray and seek my face and turn from their wicked ways, then I will hear from heaven and will forgive their sin and heal their land." (2 Chronicles 7:14)

- "He has told you, O man, what is good;
  and what does the LORD require of you but to do justice, and to love kindness,
  and to walk humbly with your God?" (Micah 6:8)

- "Whoever exalts himself will be humbled, and whoever humbles himself will be exalted." (Matthew 23:12)

- "Do nothing from selfish ambition or conceit, but in humility count others more significant than yourselves." (Philippians 2:3)

- "Have this mind among yourselves, which is yours in Christ Jesus, who, though he was in the form of God, did not count equality with God a thing to be grasped, but emptied himself, by taking the form of a servant, being born in the likeness of men. And being found in human form, he humbled himself by becoming obedient to the point of death, even death on a cross." (Philippians 2:5-8)

- "Humble yourselves before the Lord, and he will exalt you." (James 4:10)

Wow! The Bible is overwhelmingly unified in telling us that humility lies at the very heart of what it means to be fully human and to live a life surrendered to God.

Living in a posture of chosen humility doesn't mean giving up all of your sense of self, personal power, authority, convictions, and purpose.

7. Heather King, "30 Bible Verses On Having A Humble Heart." June 1, 2015, *Room to Breathe* blog, https://heathercking.org/2015/06/01/30-bible-verses-on-having-a-humble-heart/.

This is often the way humility is presented by people in power who want to keep the unempowered "in their place"; this is also one of the reasons many people in oppressed groups despise Jesus and Christianity. They blame Jesus for how Christianity gets used to suppress people's struggle for liberation, full rights, or full humanity. In case you aren't aware of it, there's a growing group of young people in the world who despise Jesus as presented by some large segments of Christianity, because they have come to see him as partner and protector of oppressors. Those of us who know the truth about Jesus must set people straight about this perversion of the image of Jesus. We have a Kingdom obligation to tell the world that, not only is Jesus not on the side of people who oppress and dehumanize others; he is opposed to them until they decide to repent.

You can't live in a posture of chosen humility, if you don't have a strong sense of self, personal power, convictions, and purpose. Humility has no power or real meaning if it's not accompanied with the option to assert privilege and seize power. Can a person who has no power, no resources, no status, no identity, no privilege, and no purpose exercise real humility? When Jesus exercised humility and washed his disciples' feet, he did it with a strong sense of his status, power, and privilege. This is how John explains the power beneath his act of humble service:

> Jesus knew that the Father had put all things under his power, and that he had come from God and was returning to God; so he got up from the meal, took off his outer clothing, and wrapped a towel around his waist. After that, he poured water into a basin and began to wash his disciples' feet, drying them with the towel that was wrapped around him. (John 13:3-5, NIV)

I call Jesus the Lion-Lamb of God. He is the Conquering Lion of Judah (Revelation 5:5), who is also the Lamb slain from the foundation of the world (Revelation 13:8). He is the perfect blend of power and meekness. He is our model for what it means to be humble. This means that the more powerful and privileged you are, the more the new community obligates you to dwell in humility.

Repentance. In many circles of Christianity, it is said repeatedly that nothing is required on our part to be *saved*. Repentance gets boiled down to a formulaic sentence that may or may not have any real spiritual essence behind it. However, repentance and humility are not statements, they are dispositions of the heart, and, while God has taken care of everything so that we can enter and experience the Kingdom, we won't be able to enter or even see the Kingdom unless we are willing to let go and give up our claims to power, status, privilege, and expertise.

We have been living in a world where hell is rampant. It has infiltrated everything from our parenting, our science, our education, our politics, and our leadership styles to our marriages, our financial decisions, our sexual practices, and our practices of self-care. In all of this, pride has set in. One of the chief sins of human beings is pride, unrelenting protection of one's ego and status:

- I know.

- This is mine.

- It's my right.

- I worked for this.

- I accomplished this.

- I earned this.

- I am entitled to this.

- I deserve this more than others.

- I've paid my dues.

- It's my turn.

- What's mine is mine.

- I have to do what's in my best interests.

- I don't need to admit when I'm wrong. I'll just do better.

- I don't change for others; others change for me.

All these statements reflect an unwillingness to change, to give up power, to unlearn, relearn, admit mistakes, own failures, apologize, or make amends. Being arrogant, uncompromising, and mean to others in our society today makes you look powerful, authoritative, and important. Society will applaud your uncompromising determination, your grit, your hardnosed demanding style, and your no-nonsense focus.

The real tragedy, however, is not that these are statements and attitudes of the captives of hell. They are the statements and attitudes of many people who represent Jesus to the world. In fact, in some wings of

Christianity, people seem to believe that an authentic Christian should never apologize, never admit to being wrong, never admit a weakness, never confess a sin, never yield to others, never give up power and privilege, and never be inconvenienced by others. Instead of using our influence to guide people toward humility and a readiness to repent, we have used our influence to help celebrate people who don't embrace these values. Because we, the Church, will not model or encourage people to live with repentance and humility, we are causing people to be in danger of self-destruction. As we love to say, "pride goes before . . . a fall" (Proverbs 16:18).

Jesus, in contrast to many people who wear his name, was always giving up power and privilege, and he never used his power for his own comfort or convenience. He was willing to look bad in order to protect the humanity of others. He was willing to put himself and his reputation at risk for the sake of bringing hope to people who were on "the wrong side of the tracks." He was always turning the power and authority of the Kingdom to the benefit of the broken, the marginalized, the rejected, and the outcasts. Jesus gave up divine status, changed, was born as a infant, and then "grew in wisdom and in stature and in favor with God and all the people" (Luke 2:52; NLT; see also Philippians 2:5-11). He had the humility to continually adjust and change to facilitate others and the divine community. His last act of ministry was to bend to his knees, in the posture of a servant, and wash his disciples' feet. He endured a horrific, painful death, giving up his life for others and the world.

The world desperately needs the Church to live into Jesus' example of humility with a willingness to repent. As America and the world teeter on the brink of chaos, the Church could be the preserving salt that could lead the world in solving major problems, if we would model and foster among others more humility and more willingness to change when confronted with new truth.

Faith

Jesus taught that faith could move mountains (Matthew 17:20; Mark 11:23), and as you know, I'm sure, this has been twisted by many in Christendom to mean things that are contrary to the character of Jesus and his new community.

Faith is not a tool to manipulate God and the universe. Faith is surrender to God's will. Faith is trusting God's Word and will with confidence that they will be fulfilled, despite evidence to the contrary. Faith isn't passive. Rather, faith sustains our actions of service to others and in the new community. We engage in acts of service with faith that God's purposes will be fulfilled. Faith is not just trusting in Jesus to get you to heaven after you die. Faith is trusting God in a way that you begin to experience heaven, now, on earth and in this life.

Faith is not superstition or magic. It is not a magical equation and supernatural formula. Faith is a matter of living from one's heart with an openness to new possibilities. Faith isn't an immunity tool that protects us from problems, pain, and afflictions. The Bible presents faith as a capacity that sustains us in the midst of pain, helps us overcome afflictions, and helps us to solve our problems. Faith isn't just about your individual salvation. It's a gift, a capacity, given to us by God to help us become faithful, creative servants in God's epic work to restore creation as a new community.

So, what is faith? How is faith to be understood if we place it in the context of the God's new community?

If hope delivers us from falling into despair, and thereby, into "hell on earth," then faith is the belief that we can overcome whatever is tempting us to despair. Faith is the capacity to believe in God's promises and plans for us and for all of creation, despite how things appear to be. When at the brink of despair, faith comes, and we begin to believe in what we have hoped for. Consider again the great verse about faith, Hebrews 11:1, "Now faith is the substance of things hoped for, the evidence of things not seen." The flow of these Kingdom virtues is so beautiful that it feels poetic, except that it is real, connected to our deepest pains and deepest struggles, and not ours alone but all of creation.

We tend to think that the opposite of faith is doubt. However, I submit that the opposite of faith is to accept false limitations. Go back to Jesus' words about how faith moves mountains. The implication of that statement is that faith helps us to overcome things that seem to be boundaries and limits to what we can do and who we can become. At so many points in his mentoring of the disciples, Jesus seemed to be saying, "Have faith. Go beyond the limits. They're not real." Observe these examples, just from the Gospel of Matthew, and look beyond the actual occurrences to the false limits that are being exposed by the power of faith:

- Faith overcomes the rules of healing. (Matthew 4:23-25)
- Faith overcomes the boundary of leprosy. (Matthew 8:1-4)
- Faith overcomes ethnic and social boundaries. (Matthew 8:1-10; 15:21-28)
- Faith overcomes fear. (Matthew 8:23-27; 10:27-31)
- Fear overcomes the powers of hell on earth. (Matthew 8:28-34)
- Faith overcomes oppressive religious rules, theological boxes, and guilt. (Matthew 9:1-8, 18-26)
- Faith overcomes blindness. (Matthew 9:27-31)
- Faith overcomes barriers to communication. (Matthew 9:32-34)
- Faith overcomes limited resources. (Matthew 14:13-21; 15:32-39)
- Faith overcomes physical limitations. (Matthew 14:22-33)
- Faith overcomes the gates of hell. (Matthew 16:17-19)

When I think about faith, I think of scarecrows! Now that I'm resident of Kansas, the analogy has taken on even more meaning. When you see a scarecrow, it means that a highly valued resource is near, and the scarecrow is there to frighten birds away from the valuable crop. Scarecrows are false dangers and false limitations. They may frighten and intimidate, but they can't really stop anything. How many starving birds have been a few feet from "prepped meals" but backed away because of a false limitation, because of something that wasn't real.

The forces of hell, discussed in the previous chapter, are gifted at setting up false limits to discourage or frighten us into despair, away from hope, or away from the treasure of God's community, especially from flourishing and mutually enriching relationships. We know that we have become tools and missional partners with these forces when we begin to do the work of creating false barriers—*scarecrows*—against, among, and between people, and between people and God.

On the contrary, one of the signs that some part of our being has been infiltrated with the power and life of the new community is when we are pressing through false barriers and false limitations of life to serve others and be good stewards of our own lives. Hebrews 11 gives us an entire list of people from the biblical story who pressed beyond the limits.

One of the reasons that Harriet Tubman is my favorite American hero is because she seemed to have developed a habit of faithfulness, relentlessly pushing through every false barrier and false limit in service of the righteous and holy mission of unchaining God's creation. She fought through slavery, brutal beatings from a childhood slave master, epilepsy, illiteracy, smallness of stature, and countless dangers to lead black slaves to freedom. She was also a spy for the Union Army and donated the land on which was constructed a home for the elderly. This summary barely scratches the surface of her remarkable life and contributions. A Methodist, Tubman obviously got the point that the faith that Jesus calls us to have is a faith that lives beyond false barriers and false limitations.[8]

If we trust God, then we will trust what God says about us and the world. If we trust that God was in Jesus, then we will trust what Jesus said about faith. Some people say they trust God with all their heart, but they won't live by faith. They are, literally, "Christian atheists." They wear the label *Christian*, but they don't live their lives by faith in God's Word. If you really trust God, then trust this:

> "Truly I tell you, if you have faith as small as a mustard seed, you can say to this mountain, 'Move from here to there,' and it will move. Nothing will be impossible for you." (Matthew 17:20; NIV)

Maybe the biggest problem with faith is that we want to operate in faith situationally. We wait for something *big* to develop in our lives, and we say to ourselves, "I'm going to walk by faith through this situation and trust God." This is not how faith is presented in the Bible. Faith

---

8. For a quick review of Tubman's life, I highly recommend these two articles: 1) Debra Michals, "Harriet Tubman." National Women's History Museum (2015), www.womenshistory.org/education-resources/biographies/harriet-tubman. 2) Biography.com Editors, "Harriet Tubman Biography," *Biography.com* (April 2, 2014), https://www.biography.com/activist/harriet-tubman

isn't a crisis-management tool or a project-management tool. Faith is something we are to live by at all times.

LOVE

You could say that humility, repentance, and faith are some of the "keys of the kingdom of heaven" (Matthew 16:19) that Jesus said belong to those who follow him. The master key, however, is *love*. In fact, love manages the other keys toward the glory of God and the well-being of God's new community.

On one occasion, a religious expert asked Jesus what he thought is the most important thing that God expects of human beings. This was Jesus' answer:

> "The first of all the commandments *is:* 'Hear, O Israel, the LORD our God, the LORD is one. And you shall love the LORD your God with all your heart, with all your soul, with all your mind, and with all your strength.' This *is* the first commandment. And the second, like *it, is* this: 'You shall love your neighbor as yourself.' There is no other commandment greater than these." (Mark 12:29-31)

To be fully human, to fulfill God's purpose of being the crown of creation, to live into the fullness of being the children of God, we must love God with all our heart, soul, mind, and strength. According to the Bible story, nothing deforms and destroys human character and being more than when we love anything more than we love God. The startling story of King Nebuchadnezzar's run in with idolatry (Daniel 3) is compelling. What an insightful story that points toward what happens when we employ our being in the service of loving something more than we love God. In this story, Nebuchadnezzar engages in the most popular form of idolatry: narcissism.

In modeling what it means to be fully human, to be creation's crown, Jesus lived a life of loving God first and foremost. His entire life was defined by relentlessly making God his top, unparalleled, and matchless priority. If we are followers of Jesus, it should be the same for us. Growing to love God with our total being is the engine of being human. Loving God isn't really a organized-religious thing, it's a human thing. It's how we become our best selves.

To follow Jesus, and to be fully human, is also to love oneself. I am super grateful that Jesus, quoting the *Shema* and Leviticus 19:18, doesn't separate loving others from loving ourselves. People who abuse, enslave, oppress, colonize, and dehumanize others in the name of God, tell their victims to love God but hate themselves, or love others, especially your oppressor or abuser, but hate yourself. How many abused women have been guilted into staying in abusive relationships because they were taught that it was wrong to prioritize and love themselves? How many have endured needless pain because, while they were busy loving the men who were abusing them, those same men were busy loving themselves?

If we follow Jesus, we discover that love of others and love of self are intertwined. Of course, we have to figure out what that looks like, but the first step is to refuse to let them be separated. They are irrevocably tied together.

A lot of chains of oppression could be broken if oppressed people would begin to love themselves as they love others.

Jesus told his disciples that love is the litmus test of authentic faith. "By this all will know that you are My disciples, if you have love for one another" (John 13:35). Paul reaffirms Jesus' words when he says that, of all the spiritual gifts that the Holy Spirit has given us to do the work of God, none is more important than love, and that without love, the other gifts become meaningless and void of purpose (1 Corinthians 13).

Think for a moment, however, about all the things that we have used to replace love as the way to test the validity or authenticity of Christian faith:

- Denominational affiliation
- Behavior in a worship service
- Speaking in tongues
- Style of dress
- Support of a particular politician
- Affiliation with a particular political party
- Size of a church building
- Volume of voice or music in worship

- Academic intelligence
- Professional success
- Wealth
- How well a person speaks or articulates
- How well someone obeys the rules of our cultural code of morality and ethics
- Use of religious or church lingo

We use everything but what Jesus said to use: love.

Now almost every Christian, if you ask her or him, will tell you that love is the measure; however, that stated belief and value doesn't get lived out in our decisions, behavior, and relationships.

I think that part of the problem is that people don't really know what Jesus means by love. I suspect that among the most sincere Christians, there's a hesitation to explore what Jesus meant for fear that there may not be anything there that makes practical sense. So we keep love at an ethereal, ideal level. We don't want Jesus to look bad, right?

A popular R&B song from the turn of the century (2000) "nailed it" in terms of how the word *love* is so over-used, misapplied, and mis-interpreted: "Love, so many people use your name in vain."[9] That's it, isn't it? This is, no doubt, why some Christians run away from the word and idea of love, looking for more functional terms to define and measure the authenticity of Christian faith and practice. Sometimes, when bearing witness to the world about Jesus, using the word *love* could be self-sabotaging. In our society, it's loaded with a lot of junk, and I do mean, a lot.

So, what did Jesus mean by love? Can we speak of a collective biblical understanding of love? Do we love God in the same way that we love ourselves and others? How can we discern if we truly love God, others, or ourselves?

Let me offer a definition of love that I think encapsulates most, if not all, of the biblical references to it; **love is service.** To love is to serve. Love is being committed to serving God and others. In loving others, we serve them to help them to live God's will for their lives. In loving

9. Andre Harris, Carvin Haggins, and Taalib Johnson, "Love," accessed November 7, 2021, https://www.lyrics.com/lyric/4183399/Love.

ourselves, we serve ourselves in a way that helps us to love into God's will for our lives.

This definition of love rescues it from being drowned out by emotions. When most of us say, "I love you," we are talking about how we *feel* about someone. What if we thought differently about love; when we say, "I love you," we mean, "I will serve you"? That would be a powerful transformation in our relationships and communities. Imagine if we switched to this meaning in our marriages, in parent-child relationships, in our friendships, and in our relationships in the new community. Emotions are not excluded or suppressed from this understanding of love. Instead of being the content of love, they become the energizer of love. That's actually what emotions are anyway. They are a form of energy. They are physiological occurrences in bodies that can provoke action once we choose to love. Thank God for giving us emotional energy to support that choice, but whether we feel it or not, as Jesus' followers, we must choose to be committed to serving God and others.

But does serving actually fulfill the command to love? Jesus said on one occasion, "If you love me, keep my commandments" (John 14:15). And we have these words, "By this all will know that you are My disciples, if you have love for one another" (John 13:35). When Jesus elaborated on the commandment to love God and love one's neighbor as we love ourselves, he told a story of a person who served another person in a dangerous situation. Jesus turned love into a deed (Luke 10:25-37). He was saying, "to love is to serve."

These words speak to the heart of Jesus, Jesus' teaching on love, and this book.

- "Anyone who claims to be in the light but hates a brother or sister is still in the darkness. Anyone who loves their brother and sister lives in the light, and there is nothing in them to make them stumble. But anyone who hates a brother or sister is in the darkness and walks around in the darkness." (1 John 2:9-11, NIV)

- "This is how we know what love is: Jesus Christ laid down his life for us. And we ought to lay down our lives for our brothers and sisters. If anyone has material possessions and sees a brother or sister in need but has no pity on them, how can the love of God be in that person? Dear children, let us not love with words or speech but with actions and in truth." (1 John 3:16-18, NIV)

- "Dear friends, let us love one another, for love comes from God. Everyone who loves has been born of God and knows God. Whoever does not love does not know God, because God is love. This is how God showed his love among us: He sent his one and only Son into the world that we might live through him. This is love: not that we loved God, but that He loved us and sent His Son as an atoning sacrifice for our sins. Dear friends, since God so loved us, we also ought to love one another. No one has ever seen God; but if we love one another, God lives in us and His love is made complete in us." (1 John 4:7-11, NIV)

- "God is love. Whoever lives in love lives in God, and God in them. This is how love is made complete among us so that we will have confidence on the day of judgment: In this world we are like Jesus. There is no fear in love. But perfect love drives out fear, because fear has to do with punishment. The one who fears is not made perfect in love." (1 John 4:16b-18, NIV)

- "We love because he first loved us. Whoever claims to love God yet hates a brother or sister is a liar. For whoever does not love their brother and sister, whom they have seen, cannot love God, whom they have not seen. And he has given us this command: Anyone who loves God must also love their brother and sister." (1 John 4:19-21, NIV)

The words of this epistle make it crystal clear that: 1) God loves us; 2) our response to God's love is to love God in return; 3) If we love God, we should love others; 4) if we don't love others, we don't love God; and 5) love is something we *do*, not just something we *feel*.

In the new community, we love God through prayer. Prayer is not a tool to manipulate or manage God. Prayer is fellowship with God, and prayer is communication with God. In prayer, we pursue God's presence. In prayer, we discover and discern God's will for others, ourselves, and God's creation. One's whole life can be lived in prayer because we can live in such a way that we remain constantly open to God's revelation of God's will. The more we pray—listen and pay attention—we become "prayer warriors" in the truest sense; that is, we become acutely aware of how God is always communicating, all around us, in all kinds of ways. As we encounter God and fellowship with God, our hearts are cultivated to love God, which means to serve God. This is what happened to Isaiah in his call story. He experiences God, is drawn closer to God, and ends up saying, "if God needs someone to serve, here am I, send me" (see Isaiah 6:1-8). When we love God more, it will be shown through service to people. The more time we spend with God, the more God's love consumes us and defines our being. We begin to live our lives as "the love of God made flesh."

No matter what people say, do, or claim, no matter how beautiful are our church buildings, worship songs, or sermons; if people aren't experiencing the love of God through us, we are defiling and desecrating the name and image of Jesus and of God in the world.

The love of God is, at least to human minds, radically inclusive. This is why the announcement about the presence of a new Kingdom, God's new Community is good news for everyone. Unlike every other kingdom, this kingdom doesn't exclude anyone who wants to enter it. In it, the sacred worth of every human being is "written in stone." The only thing that can prevent a person from entering this community is a person's own refusal to accept the offer of this amazing gift.

The radical inclusiveness of God's love and God's new community is challenging for all of us. All of us know of people who, by our judgment, are not deserving of God's love, but it's not our call to make. A good, daily meditation practice is to spend time thinking about people who you find it difficult to love (serve) and ask God to help you see their humanity. Keep on doing this daily until your vision is healed.

And never forget that, in some people's estimation, you don't deserve God's love; don't let their small-heartedness determine your destiny!

When Jesus lived among people, and he faced the same frustration and disappointments with people that we face, he chose to let love win. He chose to allow God to use his life to make a decisive statement in the world about God's love. This is the example that we must follow if we desire to be sincere followers of Jesus and if we want to experience the fullness of our humanity.

When we love people, we will pray for them. How can we know how to serve people without listening for instructions from the One who knows them best?

When we love people, we will serve them without an agenda. To love people as an expression of our love for God and God's love in us, we don't serve people to get something from them, convert them, or persuade them to see the world as we do. We love them because God loves them. Even better, we love them because the love of God is living through us. We serve and value the worth of people, even if we vehemently disagree with them and even if they are our enemies.

The call of God is upon us to live out this love-ethic. This is the defining characteristic of God's new community. This is the defining ethic and practice of people who live under the *covering* of God and the Kingdom.

When we love people, we will forgive people, as Jesus commanded. This is just personal forgiveness of people who offend us. Citizens of the new community have been given the power to apply God's forgiveness to people who need to be set free from "hell on earth." Nothing holds people in "hell on earth" more than the guilt that makes them feel that they belong there. Jesus imparts the Holy Spirit into us so that we can show up at the gates of hell and tell people the good news: "You are forgiven! You are free to leave hell. You are welcome to join us in the new community!" (see John 20:21-23)

When Jesus taught his disciples to pray, it is important to note that the only place in the prayer that refers to human action is "as we forgive our debtors." Jesus makes forgiveness the hinge upon which the door to the Kingdom opens and closes (see Matthew 6:9-14).

Conclusion

When we begin to operate the keys of the Kingdom, miracles happen. Miracles are merely signs that God's creation is being restored and evolving into God's original purpose for it. Miracles aren't things that aren't supposed to happen. Miracles are the signs pointing to the way life in God's creation is supposed to be. Miracles are the symptoms of renewal and restoration. Miracles are the truth about how we are "bubbling up" out of oblivion! This is why Jesus was never astonished by miracles. He expected them. For Jesus, what we call miraculous is merely proof that the glory of God is all over God's creation!

11
JESUS CROWNED

If Jesus had been killed twenty years ago, Catholic school children would be wearing little electric chairs around their necks instead of crosses.

—*Lenny Bruce*[1]

S o, now we come to what the Gospels saw as the crux of Jesus' life: his crucifixion, resurrection, and ascension.

Crucifixion

The New Testament points collectively toward an understanding of the crucifixion of Jesus as connected to the sacrificial system of ancient Israelite faith, a way to heal the sins of human beings, and we accept this joyfully in faith. Jesus' sacrificial death defeated the kingdom of darkness and claimed our destiny in ways that we will never fully understand. I deeply appreciate most of the various theories of atonement, so long as they lead to a life of self-sacrificing service to God and others.

I do think, however, that some parts of Christendom have an obsession with the brutal details of Jesus' crucifixion, as if to say that the power of his crucifixion is in the depth of the pain. This implies that, had the pain been less severe, it would have been less effective in accomplishing God's will, and we wouldn't need to be as grateful. This

1. Lenny Bruce Quotes. BrainyQuote.com, BrainyMedia Inc, 2022. https://www.brainyquote.com/quotes/lenny_bruce_107553, accessed January 7, 2022

seems to have been the emphasis of Mel Gibson's movie, *The Passion of the Christ*. At least, that was the reaction to the movie that I kept hearing from people who saw it. People were saying that the movie was powerful and transformative because it displayed the depth of Jesus' suffering. Furthermore, I have seen this in churches all my life. It is part of the practice of preachers in most of the church circles I have been in to make a plea for Christian commitment based on "how much Jesus suffered for you." I am not sure this is healthy or helpful.

The crucial aspects of Jesus' life must be interpreted in the context of the new community that Jesus came to launch. If we do that, some astonishing truths come to surface.

The crucifixion happened because God determined that we and the rest of creation are worth dying for.

Jesus' crucifixion shows the depth of the evil that opposed him and that opposes God and the new community. When one kingdom overtakes another, there is almost always violence. From the moment Jesus arrived, there was violence, from Herod's massacre of Israelite boys to the crucifixion.

Jesus' crucifixion shows the depth of the evil that develops in human hearts that have deserted the call to full humanity and have resorted instead to lives of amassing wealth, power, and ego-boosts. When the idols of wealth, power, and pride converge in human souls and human systems, they become a demonic stronghold that will feel threatened by anything and anyone pointing toward self-sacrificing love, self-love, service, humility, community, repentance, or faith. I once heard the great business guru, Peter Drucker, say that "culture eats vision for lunch." This is what happens in any culture that has been structured around accumulating wealth, power, and supplements to arrogance. When a vision for truth, love, justice, and community is introduced into such a culture, the culture will engage in all-out war to destroy it. This is one of the reasons Jesus was crucified.

Jesus' crucifixion happened because he rattled the cage of the religious system into which he was born, calling for that system to be more just and more humane. The well-known secret of church culture is that some of the strongest anti-Kingdom, anti-Jesus strongholds in our society are in local churches. To challenge people's religious systems and practices is to invite hatred and war. There is, probably, no demonic force like that of an evil adorned in religious devotion. I could tell you a thousand tales of it, and to see it can be frightening to even the bravest among us. For example, can you imagine what sounds of "screaming demons" we would hear if those churches in America that engage in bullying homosexuals would decide, instead, to "pull off the covers" on adultery, fornication, unforgiveness, idolatry, racism, unbridled greed, or neglect of the poor? Go into any community in America, and often, some of the deepest evils in the community will be those that have found a place to hide within local churches.

The crucifixion happened because God in Jesus was uniting with us in our sickness, pain, and suffering, especially those among us who suffer unjustly. Since the crucifixion, untold millions of people who experience suffering have found the strength to endure and overcome the temptation to despair because they considered Jesus' suffering, the suffering of Immanuel—God with us—and they knew that God was with them in their pain. In this, they found hope.

God didn't just enter into our suffering in Jesus. Through Jesus, God defeated the sin, evil, and dark powers that seek to destroy us and oppose God's Creation.

The crucifixion of Jesus happened because God was saying decisively what has always been true: God loves us with an everlasting love. Contrary to how the message of Jesus' crucifixion is often presented, God didn't start loving and forgiving us at Calvary. God has always loved us. At Calvary, God was expressing God's love. Calvary has the power to provoke hope, the kind of hope that keeps people from giving in to despair and falling into "hell on earth." Calvary has the power to provoke faith, the kind of faith pushes beyond the limits to serve others and build God's new community.

The crucifixion of Jesus happened because it was an unveiling of the eternal truth about the nature of life and all reality. While he was exiled on Patmos Island, an early follower of Jesus named John was given an exceptional and extraordinary gift. The Creator pulled back the curtain of reality to let him see the unadorned and unfiltered truth, the essential power that rules the destiny of all life. And what did John see? A mighty military? A dominating imperial establishment? An inarguable intellectual system? A pervasive technological and scientific creation? No, John saw none of those things. He saw a slain lamb from the foundation of the world. The crucifixion was revealing life's essential truth. Life is moved forward through self-sacrificing service. It is no wonder that

Matthew records that, at the moment of Jesus' death, there was a violent reaction in the earth and in the Temple; all of reality was being rocked by confrontation with the fundamental truth about life. This truth had to cause violence as it collided with a world system that had been taken over and dominated by unconstrained power, unbridled greed, and unchecked pride and arrogance. The kingdom of darkness was taken down by a slaughtered lamb!

Jesus' death was the decisive battle for our souls and all of creation, and in submitting to this purpose, Jesus became, truly, the crown of creation. By becoming one with the eternal truth, Jesus took on the crown of the Lamb!

Resurrection

Jesus was also *crowned* through his resurrection. Having defeated the powers of death and the grave, he arose, Lord of all, in possession of all authority:

> Then Jesus came to them and said, "All authority in heaven and on earth has been given to me." (Matthew 28:18, NIV)

The resurrection is proof that what God was doing through Jesus, at Calvary, worked. Jesus had faced the powers of death, evil, despair, sin, and destructions, and he won. Like miracles, Jesus' resurrection is proof that creation is being restored and growing into the "New Jerusalem" (Revelation 21). The forces of darkness are trying to suppress the revolution against them, but the revolution keeps "bubbling up" through the darkness. Jesus' resurrection was the ultimate outbreak of God's insurrection!

Some theologians, such as N.T. Wright in his book, *Surprised by Hope*, view Jesus' resurrection as God's ultimate sign of hope. As mentioned in the previous chapter, hope keeps us from falling into despair and allowing the powers of evil to pull us into "hell on earth." If all the powers and energies of evil conspired to destroy Jesus, who was God's decisive message and ultimate restorative act, but God overcame the full onslaught of evil and raised Jesus from death and the grave, then all of creation can dwell in hope. That's why it is so important that the body of Christ, the Church, proclaim the resurrection every day relentlessly. All creation must be made aware and reminded of the hope we have through the resurrection of Jesus. There is nothing we will ever face that is stronger than God's power to restore, rebuild, sustain, strengthen, not even death.

The resurrection also inspires faith, because it inspires us to believe God beyond the false limits that have been set up by the powers of evil. Christians have to stop withdrawing from the resurrection, fearing that it will be deemed irrelevant by the world or an outdated myth. Yet all around us, people are looking for and celebrating stories of comeback, redemption, and triumph over disaster, because they want to believe that they too can overcome all that has come against them in life. They want to be inspired to believe that they can overcome the limits that they know are restraining them from their best lives. Hollywood gets this. Sometimes, it seems that the Church does not. We have the greatest comeback story of all time, and it's not just a fictional story created by Hollywood. Rather, it is the story at the center of all reality. The resurrection of Jesus needs to be celebrated more than once a year at Easter and placed at the very center of all that we do and say. Everything that happens in a local church should reflect faith that is inspired by the resurrection, from our budgets to our banquets!

The crucifixion and the resurrection must be proclaimed together. We must tell the world about, and live out, these two vital truths: Jesus-Crucified, and Jesus-Resurrected! The two occurrences belong together. They interpret each other. Together, they present a full summation of the biblical story. The crucifixion displays to us the powers of evil and darkness and how they conspired to destroy God's creation. The resurrection displays to us how God overcame, and is overcoming, the powers of evil and darkness. The resurrection will not be appreciated if it is separated from the crucifixion. The crucifixion can be twisted into an obsession with suffering if it isn't connected to the resurrection. The power of Jesus resurrected is that he overcame the crucifixion.

In African American churches, especially among Baptists, there is a long-held tradition that you never preach without "putting Jesus on the cross" and "raising Jesus out of the grave." Maybe this is why the black Christian faith experience is so gifted at abounding in hope.

When you consider the full story of black people's experience in America, it is astonishing that we have survived. It is a story that is so dark and so evil that, right now as I write, there are people trying to prevent it from being taught in public schools as part of the essential history of America. "It will make white children feel guilty for something they didn't do, and it will make black children see themselves as victims," so the argument goes. The story of black people in America is of such profound suffering that just to tell it is considered revolutionary. Imagine having lived it!

Part of the reason black people have survived is because of the hope and faith received in black churches. Long before our preachers had training in theology, exegesis, hermeneutics, pastoral counseling, and leadership development, we had one thing that we did well and that sustained our people in the worst of circumstances: the crucifixion and the resurrection. Why did that work? How did our people survive and thrive in a world defined by slavery, bondage, lynchings, exclusion, degradation, mass incarceration, and daily desolation? They overcame because, before they had anything else, they had the hope and faith generated from the story of the "brown-skin brother" who was unjustly convicted, placed on death-row, crucified, and buried in a borrowed tomb; but early on that following Sunday morning, he rose from death and the grave, claiming all power and authority on earth and in heaven! If hope can be maintained and faith can be ignited, love is empowered. Then miracles will break out all around us as signs of God's new creation consume the world!

Ascension

The Gospels tell us that, after the resurrection, Jesus ascended into the heavens, something that we can barely grasp because it transcends our understanding of God's full reality. This transition, however, became the third crowning of Jesus. In his ascension, we are told by the New Testament writers that Jesus is "at the right hand of God" (Acts 7:55-56; Hebrews 1:3; 12:2; 1 Peter 3:22). Bible scholars tell us that this means that God has placed Jesus in the seat of authority as the judge of all creation. This cannot be fully understood by our minds, and it need not be. What is most important to grasp is that it means that God measures all things by Jesus. This is why we can never again separate the crucified and risen Lord from the life he lived as the Word made flesh. We will be measured by that life. That life is the measure of full humanity. That life is the measure of what it means to be the Church. To become that life in our world is the goal of Christian faith. Paul says that God is measuring the restoration project by Jesus. The closer we, the crowns of creation, get to reflecting the image of Jesus, the closer we'll be to the full redemption of creation.

Jesus told his disciples that, after his departure, the Holy Spirit would come to remind us of what Jesus said and did and to reveal more things that transcend the life of Jesus on earth (John 16:12-14). The Holy Spirit is present with us, helping us to live, bear witness to, and walk with Jesus.

A Closing Prayer: Take These Chains from My Heart

Holy Spirit, break the chains we have placed upon ourselves through our distorted and perverted images of Jesus, his mission, and his message. As we are unchained from our idols, may we see Jesus as he truly is, the Light of the world!

Help us to open our lives to Jesus so that he may come and freely live in and through us.

Help us to grow in our love for Jesus without trying to own him or bend him to our selfish pursuits.

May we join him in seeking to fulfill the blessing of Abraham, to be a blessing to all people!

May we faithfully bear witness to Jesus, our crucified and risen Lord, the one who claims total victory over all the forces of evil and invites us to join him both in his victory and in God's new community! Amen!

CPSIA information can be obtained
at www.ICGtesting.com
Printed in the USA
LVHW101204060522
718086LV00031B/1007

9 781953 495310